A
DICTIONARY
FOR UNITED METHODISTS

A
DICTIONARY
FOR
UNITED
METHODISTS

ALAN K. WALTZ

Abingdon Press
Nashville

A DICTIONARY FOR UNITED METHODISTS

Copyright © 1991 by Abingdon Press

This book is printed on acid-free paper.

Library of Congress Cataloging-in-Publication Data

Waltz, Alan K.
A dictionary for United Methodists / Alan K. Waltz.
p. cm.
Includes bibliographical references.
ISBN 0-687-10754-7 (alk. paper)
1. United Methodist Church (U.S.)–Government–Dictionaries.
2. United Methodist Church (U.S.)–Liturgy–Dictionaries.
3. Methodist Church–United States–Government–Dictionaries.
4. Methodist Church–United States–Liturgy–Dictionaries.
I. Title.
BX8382.2.Z5W34 1991
262'.076'03–dc20   90-44117
                                                                              CIP

Pronunciations are from Webster's *Ninth New Collegiate Dictionary* © 1964
Merriam-Webster. Springfield, Mass.: Merriam-Webster, Inc., Publishers.

MANUFACTURED IN THE UNITED STATES OF AMERICA

CONTENTS

Introduction 7

United Methodist Organizational
   and Worship Terms..13

Acronyms and Abbreviations in Use in
   The United Methodist Church 199

Reference Materials for
   Additional Reading..207

INTRODUCTION

Why should a dictionary of organizational and worship terms that are widely used in The United Methodist Church be compiled? Could United Methodists simply go to any good dictionary, or perhaps in some cases to an unabridged one, and find the meanings of the terms included here? Do United Methodists have distinct words and meanings for the words they use in order to understand and discuss organizational and worship life?

The fact is that unique meanings and understandings have grown up over the years for many words and phrases that United Methodists routinely use. Often it is assumed within our fellowship that everyone at the local, Annual Conference, and national levels of the denomination knows what the basic meaning of a commonly used term is or the specific connotation it holds for United Methodists. Persons who have been members of The United Methodist Church may be familiar with the terms and their meanings. As a result these United Methodists are comfortable in their understandings of how and why we do things in the church. Many of our members who are or have been leaders have learned the "language" of the local church or the denomination. They tend to assume all members share their depth of knowledge and understanding.

Today, however, many of our members have not been United Methodists very long. They are either younger persons or have joined our fellowship by profession of faith in Christ or through transfer from another Christian denomination. These persons may have only a cursory knowledge of our history and form of church government. Unless there is specific reason to do so, most worship practices and church government policies are never taught or explained in detail. So discussion is hampered by the lack of a shared understanding of even the words we use together as United Methodists.

This dictionary has been compiled to facilitate communication among members by providing a succinct definition of the vocabulary we use in our life together as United Methodists. If communication and understanding are improved, our worship and organizational experiences will have greater significance for all of us.

Four presuppositions underlie the plan of this book.

1) Some of the organizational and worship terms used in United Methodism have meanings and nuances distinct to our denomination. Sometimes, the basic word and definition can be found in a standard dictionary, but through the passage of time and custom the words have acquired a singular import and usage unique in The United Methodist Church.

2) Many United Methodists have forgotten or were never informed about the distinctive character of our church and the way in which we talk about its customs

and practices. As a consequence, we are often not able to share fully the significance of worship or understand completely conversation about the processes of church government.

3) Many of today's members did not grow up within The United Methodist Church. Some came as adults into our fellowship with no background in our church. Others grew up in other Christian communions, with different traditions. These persons often find that the United Methodist understanding of a word differs significantly from what they previously understood it to mean.

4) Because we come together as a people committed to Christ and share in the particular expression of that faith which is found in United Methodism, we need to be able to share meaningfully that expression of faith. A shared understanding of our heritage as reflected in the terms we use will enable us to more clearly communicate among ourselves both in the local church and in the broader arenas of the denomination.

Let me briefly tell you what you will and will not find in this dictionary.

1) The list of the items included has been shaped by the very character of United Methodism. Our worship life together has not been shaped by the form and detail of ritual and observance, which has characterized other denominations such as the Roman Catholic Church, the Episcopal Church, and the Orthodox churches. Rather United Methodism in America has been shaped by the historical emphasis upon preaching, on the simple but meaningful observance of the sacraments, and upon the faith response of the individual Christian.

2) Much of the distinctive character of United Methodism is found in its polity, its form of church government. It is unique in its emphasis upon "the connection," the holding together of all parts of the denomination for the common good. It is also unique in its pattern of deploying or appointing pastors to fields of service, a system called the itineracy.

In consequence, United Methodism understands itself more in terms of the distinctive character of its organizational life than in distinctive practices of worship or singular emphases of doctrine. Because this is the case, two-thirds of the entries in this dictionary relate to the organization and polity of The United Methodist Church and only one-third relates to worship concepts.

3) The dictionary has been designed to provide concise definitions of terms as they are currently used. It does not seek to trace word etymologies. In some cases a brief background is given to aid in understanding current usage.

4) This dictionary is not an official United Methodist resource. Nor is it unabridged. The intent has been to include those words which are current in the denomination and most important to an understanding of United Methodism by lay persons and clergy in the local churches.

5) This volume has been designed as a reference that can be easily and readily used. The intent has been to provide succinct definitions that are not technical or complex.

6) No attempt has been made to provide a detailed or scholarly treatment of each term. This book is a dictionary in the sense of the following definition: a reference book listing terms and names along with their mean-

ings and applications. If detailed expositions are desired, other resources should be explored.

7) This dictionary does not attempt to define theological terms of importance to Christians in general or to United Methodists in particular.

8) With only five exceptions, not included are biographical references to persons of historical importance to United Methodism. The five exceptions are persons of historical importance in the founding of the predecessor denominations that now compose The United Methodist Church.

Two additional resources are provided for the reader. The first is a listing of acronyms and abbreviations currently in wide use in The United Methodist Church. The second is a brief listing of resources for those who may wish to read further on the entries.

I am deeply grateful for the assistance of two persons who have been especially helpful in the work on this dictionary. Its contents have been considerably strengthened by their review. Hoyt L. Hickman (Director, Resource Development, Section on Worship, General Board of Discipleship) has reviewed both the list and content of the worship entries. His counsel is highly prized because of his long experience in and great knowledge about worship in our denomination. Robert L. Wilson (Professor of Church and Society, The Divinity School, Duke University) has reviewed the list of entries and the definitions for the entire manuscript. He has been a student and teacher of the organizational life of United Methodism for many years, and his wisdom and guidance are deeply appreciated. Any deficiencies in this volume must not be ascribed to these two distinguished scholars and friends, but solely to me.

I hope this dictionary will commend itself to you. If it improves our shared understanding of the vocabulary of our denomination it will have served its purpose. Through that enhanced understanding, it is hoped that the life and ministry in Christ we share together as United Methodists will be enriched.

Alan K. Waltz

UNITED METHODIST ORGANIZATIONAL
AND WORSHIP TERMS

abandon, local church. The formal process of disposing of the property and other assets of a local church when a congregation has disbanded and no longer continues to meet. In United Methodist usage, the term *abandon* means that the Annual Conference no longer has an interest in maintaining the property for local church purposes. Because the title to the property of all United Methodist churches is held in trust for the Annual Conference, it must take the final action to dispose of the property. The recommendation for this action comes from the presiding bishop, at least a majority of the district superintendents, and the district Board of Church Location and Building. Following such action, the Annual Conference trustees assume control of the property. The permanent records of the local church are to be maintained properly and the property transferred or sold.

Abingdon Press. The name used by The United Methodist Publishing House for the publishing of books. The name is connected with American Methodism through the founding of Cokesbury College in Abingdon, Maryland. The college was short-lived

(1787–1795). In 1915 the name Abingdon Press was first adopted by the Methodist Book Concern of The Methodist Episcopal Church. In 1923, The Methodist Episcopal Church, South, adopted Cokesbury as the name for the book publishing department of its publishing house. At the time of the 1939 union, Abingdon-Cokesbury was adopted as the trade name. This was used until 1954 when Abingdon was designated as the name for the church press and Cokesbury was used as the name for the retail unit operated by The United Methodist Publishing House.

accountability. One of two words (the other being *amenability*) used in a precise way to define the relationships between organizational units of The United Methodist Church. Accountability is the requirement of an organized structural unit to report, explain, or justify its action or actions to another unit in the denomination. The requirement also implies a willingness to receive from and give careful consideration to references and recommendations made by the unit to which it is accountable. *The Book of Discipline* provides that all program-related general agencies of The United Methodist Church are accountable to the General Council on Ministries between sessions of the General Conference. Agencies receiving monies appropriated by the General Conference are accountable to the General Council on Finance and Administration for the budgeting, financial accounting, and utilization of these funds.

See also *amenability*.

acolyte. A person who assists in the worship service. Normally the acolyte serves by lighting and extinguishing the candles on the communion or altar table and distributing and collecting offering plates. At the discretion of the pastor, the acolyte may also assist in other portions of the worship service. It is the custom in most local churches for the acolytes to be young persons, giving them an early opportunity to be participants in the service. Adults, however, also may serve as acolytes.

Act of Covenanting. The mutual agreement of an autonomous Methodist church and The United Methodist Church to enter into a relationship with each other. The Act of Covenanting includes a mutual recognition of baptism and ordination, full participation of members of each in Holy Communion, and a commitment to finding new relationships in program and outreach.

See also *Affiliated Autonomous Methodist Church.*

Administrative Board. The primary administrative body of the local church. It has general oversight of the administration and program. It devises plans and goals, establishes the budget, ensures the promotion of the benevolence causes, sets the salaries of staff, and carries other responsibilities given to it by the Charge Conference. The Administrative Board is amenable to the Charge Conference.

See also *Charge Conference.*

Administrative Council. A body with the combined responsibilities of the Administrative Board and the Council on Ministries. It is an alternative organizational pattern and is designed especially for small membership churches. It provides all the planning and implementation of the program life of the church as well as the administration of the organization. The

17

Administrative Council is amenable to the Charge Conference.

See also *Charge Conference.*

administrative location of ordained ministers.

The process by which an ordained minister may be removed from the itinerant ministry, that is, no longer given a pastoral appointment, because of an inability to perform effectively the duties of a minister. Administrative location is accomplished by vote of the ministerial members of an Annual Conference upon the recommendation of the Board of Ordained Ministry.

See also *location of clergy, administrative.*

admission into the church.

See *membership, local church.*

Advance for Christ and His Church, The.

A program of benevolence giving of The United Methodist Church for more than forty years. Denomination-wide, projects are approved to receive special gifts for missions and relief in the United States and throughout the world. These funds are disbursed by the General Board of Global Ministries in accordance with procedures established by the Advance Committee of the General Council on Ministries.

A similar program for benevolence projects exists in the Annual Conference for mission and outreach programs.

Advance special gifts.

Gifts given to projects approved as a part of the benevolence program known as The Advance for Christ and His Church. Advance special gifts are given to approved projects at the denominational and Annual Conference levels. These are gifts contributed in addition to the apportioned World Service and conference benevolence funds. Local United Methodist churches receive special notice and credit for monies given for Advance special projects.

Advent. Since the eighth century, the beginning or first season of the Christian year. Advent focuses on preparing for the coming of Christ. The term is derived from the Latin word *adventus*, meaning to come. The season or period of Advent always includes the four Sundays before Christmas Day. (It begins with the Sunday closest to November 30 and ends with Christmas Eve day.) Because December 25 does not always fall on the same day of the week, the number of days in the Advent season varies from year to year. The liturgical color for Advent is purple.

Advent wreath. Wreaths used during the observance of Advent. Advent wreaths are of two basic types. The first is a circle, generally of evergreens, which is hung in the sanctuary of the church as part of the special decorations for the Advent season. Wreaths of evergreen and other materials are increasingly used during Advent to decorate the exterior doors of churches and of people's homes.

The other basic form of the Advent wreath is that of a circle holding four candles. Generally the color of all four candles is purple (although it is an increasing practice for the third candle to be pink or rose). These candles are lit in a special sequence during worship services on the four Sundays of Advent. A candle is lighted on the first Sunday of Advent, and on each successive Sunday an additional candle is lit.

In recent years it has become customary to have a

larger white candle in the center of the Advent wreath. This is often called the "Christ candle" and is lit at the Christmas Eve services and on Christmas Day.

Small Advent wreaths have served as the center of family devotions through Advent. In private or home use, the first candle is lit the first Sunday and every day until Christmas; the second candle is lit on the second Sunday and every day following and so on.

See also *Christ candle.*

Advocate, The Christian. A historic name in publishing for The United Methodist Church and its predecessor denominations. In 1826 *The Christian Advocate* was begun as a newspaper for American Methodism. Over time it combined and merged with other publications. Regional and Annual Conference editions developed through the 1800s. With the division of The Methodist Episcopal Church in 1844, separate editions were published. With the 1939 union of the Methodist bodies, a central publication was established. In 1956, *The New Christian Advocate* was developed as a publication for the clergy. This was discontinued in the early 1970s and has been replaced by *The Circuit Rider,* also primarily for the clergy. The name Christian Advocate remains as a part of the title for a few Annual Conference papers. It is also used as *The Daily Christian Advocate,* which is the publication of information for the General Conference. *The Daily Christian Advocate* now serves as the official journal for the General Conference.

Affiliated Autonomous Methodist Church. A self-governing Methodist Church outside the United States. Examples of such churches are The Methodist Church of Chile and The Methodist Church of Korea. Historically, the establishment of an Affiliated

Autonomous Methodist Church has been assisted by The United Methodist Church or one of its predecessor denominations (The Evangelical United Brethren Church and The Methodist Church). In addition, an Affiliated Autonomous Methodist Church has by mutual agreement entered into a covenant of relationship or an Act of Covenanting with The United Methodist Church.

See also *Act of Covenanting.*

affiliate member of a local church (lay). A lay person residing away from home for an extended period who is enrolled in a nearby church for fellowship, pastoral care, and participation in activities. The affiliate member may hold office, except for those that would place him or her on the Administrative Board or Council. The affiliate member is still counted as a member of the home church.

affiliate member of an Annual Conference (ministerial). An ordained minister serving in an appointment outside the Annual Conference in which membership is held who has been granted an affiliate relationship with the Annual Conference in which the appointment is located. The minister may initiate the relationship by applying to the Board of Ordained Ministry for affiliate membership in the Annual Conference in which the ministerial appointment is located. Upon recommendation by the Board of Ordained Ministry, the affiliate relationship is granted by a vote of the ministerial members of the Annual Conference. If the affiliate membership is granted, then the minister has the right to serve on Conference boards and agencies with voice but not vote. Voting membership is retained in the minister's home Annual Conference.

affirmation of faith. A creed or a series of statements by which Christians declare their belief in the core doctrines. Usually the affirmations are used in the local church worship services. Although they do not serve as statements of required belief (as do creeds or confessions of faith in some denominations), the affirmations of faith do reflect the broad United Methodist understanding of the core doctrines. Affirmations of faith commonly used in The United Methodist Church are The Apostles' Creed, The Nicene Creed, The Korean Creed, and affirmations from the Scriptures.

age-level, family, and specialized-ministries coordinators. Persons elected annually by the local United Methodist church Charge Conference to represent the concerns of a particular age level when they are not otherwise represented in the Council on Ministries or Administrative Council. The Charge Conference may elect a coordinator of children's ministries, a coordinator of youth ministries, a coordinator of adult ministries, and a coordinator of family ministries as needed. They study the needs of the age group and coordinate the planning and implementation of a unified ministry for the age level within the total program and life of the congregation.

age-level and family councils. Organizational units in the local church established by the Council on Ministries or the Administrative Council. The number of age-level and family councils in a local church depends upon the size of the congregation and the extent of the program. These councils work under the leadership of the age-level and family coordinators to plan for and facilitate an integrated program throughout the local church for persons of various ages.

agencies, Annual Conference. The councils, boards, commissions, committees, task forces, or any other body established by an Annual Conference to carry out its work. These agencies are to provide for the connectional relationship between the general agencies and the Conference, districts, and local churches.

agencies, general. A term used generically to refer to any council, board, commission, committee, or other units established to carry out the work of the denomination. General agencies are accountable to the General Conference.

alb. A vestment worn by persons taking leadership roles in worship services. It is a full-length white garment. It may be gathered at the waist by a rope or cloth

band. In recent years some United Methodist ordained and diaconal ministers, lay assistants, choirs, and acolytes have begun wearing the alb in services of worship.

See also *cincture.*

Albright (Albrecht), Jacob. Founder of the Evangelical branch of The Evangelical United Brethren Church. Albright (1759–1808), a native of Pennsylvania, grew up in the Reformed Church. In his early adult life he was greatly influenced by a Methodist class meeting, which eventually licensed him as an exhorter, a lay preacher in Methodism. He began to preach to his German neighbors and was soon traveling through Pennsylvania preaching in many places. By 1807, he held his first conference of three preachers and a membership of two hundred. The work he began grew and formed The Evangelical Church, which in 1946 merged with the Church of the United Brethren in Christ to form The Evangelical United Brethren Church.

Aldersgate. From Aldersgate Street in London. On this street was a meeting place in which John Wesley had his heart-warming conversion experience on May 24, 1739. Charles Wesley only a few days before had also had a conversion experience in the same place. The building where the meetings took place no longer exists. Aldersgate Street has been shortened by common Methodist usage to simply Aldersgate. The word has come to represent both the place and the experience.

alleluia, hallelujah. Expressions of praise and joy used in worship services and hymns. Hallelujah is from the Hebrew word meaning "praise God." Alleluia is the Latin form of the same word.

altar. Historically, an altar has been the table or structure on which a sacrifice is offered. In the liturgical Christian groups, such as the Roman Catholic and Orthodox churches, the altar has been the table upon which the bread and wine are placed during the celebration of the Mass. For liturgical denominations the Mass represents again the sacrifice of Christ for the world.

Strictly speaking, United Methodists do not have an altar in this sense. The Methodist tradition has been to have a Lord's table or communion table upon which the elements are placed during the service of Holy Communion. In recent years, with the building of United Methodist churches with "divided chancels," the communion table has often been referred to, albeit incorrectly, as the altar.

The word *altar* has been used in another way in United Methodist tradition. Often, those in the congregation are invited to come to the altar for prayer or for special services such as baptism or reception into membership. Here the usage means that people are to come to the chancel rail. Altar in this sense has a symbolic meaning.

altar call. The invitation offered by the pastor to come forward to the chancel rail or communion table in order to dedicate one's life to Christ, to become a member of the congregation, or to offer prayer.

altar cloth. The cloth which covers the Lord's table or communion table. When only one color is used throughout the year, it is usually white. In many churches the color of the cloth is changed to reflect the various seasons of the Christian year.

See also *paraments.*

25

altar guild. A group of lay persons in the church who are responsible for the care and decorating of the chancel area including the communion table or altar. This group, often organized into a standing committee, changes the altar cloths or paraments as needed. It is also responsible for providing an arrangement of flowers, placed on the communion table or altar. In some congregations this group also includes the communion stewards.

altar railing or rail.
See *chancel railing or rail.*

Amen. From the Hebrew and Greek words meaning certainly or truly. It has been used in the sense of "So be it." It is commonly used as the closing word or affirmation of hymns and as the usual closing for public and private prayer. In congregational services of worship, the use of *Amen* provides a means for the congregation to affirm the prayer or statement of faith just given by the worship leader.

amenability. One of two words (the other being *accountability*) used in a precise way to define the relationship between organizational units of The United Methodist Church. Amenability is the requirement of an organized unit to answer to, act under instruction of, agree with, yield to, or submit to another unit in the church structure. It connotes legal responsibility. *The Book of Discipline* states that all general agencies of The United Methodist Church that have been constituted by the General Conference are amenable to the General Conference, except as otherwise provided. In the local church, the various committees and work units are amenable to the Charge Conference.

See also *accountability.*

American Bible Society. The organization in the United States which translates, prints, and distributes the Bible throughout the world. The American Bible Society is recognized by The United Methodist Church as a means of mission outreach and receives some financial support from denominational funds as well as contributions from local churches.

Anglican. The word often used to refer to The Church of England as well as other denominations worldwide connected with The Church of England. *Anglicanism* is the word used to describe the claim of The Church of England to represent a body of Christendom distinct from Roman Catholic, Orthodox, and Protestant traditions. Anglicans are members of these churches, which include the Episcopal Church in the United States. Members of this latter church normally refer to themselves as Episcopalians rather than as Anglicans. John Wesley, the founder of Methodism, was a lifelong member of The Church of England.

See also *Church of England, The.*

Annual Conference. The basic organizational body in The United Methodist Church. An Annual Conference includes all United Methodist churches in a geographically defined area. Lay and ministerial members of the Annual Conference have the right to vote on all constitutional amendments and delegates to General and Jurisdictional Conferences. Members establish the budget for the Annual Conference and vote on all matters related to the organizational life of its agencies and institutions. The Annual Conference members are responsible for the program and administration of the work of the Annual Conference and its local churches. Only ministerial members vote on all matters relating to ministerial membership and ordination. The membership of the Annual Conference consists of an equal number of lay and clergy members, and at least one lay person from each pastoral charge is to be a member.

Annual Conference agencies.
See *agencies, Annual Conference.*

anthem. A hymn or choral work sung by a choir or musical group such as a quartet. The anthem as an act of praise and glorification of God is sung to lead the congregation in worship. The anthem is an integral part of most United Methodist Sunday worship services.

Apocrypha. The collective name given to the collection of fifteen books written generally during the period between the writing of the last books of the Old Testament and those of the New Testament. The word *apocrypha* literally means "things that are hidden." When the canon or official list of books was established for the Jews (the Old Testament) these books were not included. A Greek translation of the Old Testament books, however, known as the Septuagint, which circulated widely in the early Christian church, did include the books. The Roman Catholic Church and the Eastern Orthodox Churches recognize these books as authoritative.

Protestants have not recognized the books of the Apocrypha as Scripture or authoritative; therefore, they are not included in most Bibles used by Protestants. If the Apocrypha is printed at all, it is as a separate section and is included in recognition of the use made by other groups and for the information it contains concerning the period between those of the Old and New Testaments.

Reading from the Apocrypha is now an option in the commonly used lectionaries.

Apostles' Creed. The affirmation of faith most widely used by United Methodists. The Apostles' Creed derives its name from its use in the Christian church from as early as A.D. 150 and the early belief that it was used by the apostles. Beginning in the third century, this creed was used at baptisms by the Roman Catholic Church. Through the years it has been used widely by both Roman Catholics and Protestants as the formative statement of the faith into which Christians are baptized.

appeal. A part of the detailed judicial procedures in The United Methodist Church available to ministers and lay persons against whom charges are brought under the provisions of *The Book of Discipline*.

The trial and judicial process provides for a number of levels of trials and appeals. The highest of these is the Judicial Council, which has the final word.

One of the fundamental rights in the judicial process is that of an appeal to the next higher level. This right of appeal is provided for in the Constitution of The United Methodist Church as one of the Restrictive Rules.

See also *Restrictive Rules, the.*

appointment, ministerial. The annual assignment to a field of service of ministerial members active in an Annual Conference. The appointment may be to a pastoral charge or to special appointments beyond the local church. Only those ministerial members who are retired or who have been granted a sabbatical leave, a disability leave, or a leave of absence do not receive an appointment.

The clergy deployment system for The United Methodist Church is referred to as the itinerant system. Under this system ordained ministers are appointed or sent by the bishop to their assignments. It is the obligation of the ministerial members to accept these appointments.

The term is also often applied to the place or position to which the ordained minister has been assigned by the bishop.

See also *itineracy, itinerancy.*

appointment, service. The appointment given annually to all diaconal ministers who are in good standing in an Annual Conference. A service appointment is negotiated by the employing agency or unit and the diaconal minister. It is then recommended by the conference Board of Diaconal Ministry, reviewed by the Cabinet, and approved by the bishop. All diaconal ministers, except those who are retired, on a sabbatical or disability leave, or a leave of absence, must have a service appointment to maintain their credentials as diaconal ministers.

appointment beyond the local church. An appointment of an ordained minister by a bishop to an assignment or ministry setting other than a local church. Appointments beyond the local church include service as hospital and military chaplains, staff of Annual Conference and general agencies, missionaries, and specialized ministries. These ministers are subject to annual appointment and review and must remain willing to accept an appointment to a pastoral charge if this be the desire of the bishop.

appointment to a pastoral charge. The appointment by a bishop of an ordained minister (or a person licensed and approved by the ministerial members of an Annual Conference) to serve one or more local churches in the Annual Conference. The minister is appointed to oversee the breadth of the ministry of the local church, to preach, to administer the Sacraments, to minister to the members and the community, and to administer the work of the church.

apportionment. An amount assigned to a local church, Annual Conference, or other United Methodist body by a proper church authority to be raised as its share of a church fund. For example, the General Conference establishes the budget for the various general funds of the denomination. These are then apportioned on the basis of a specific formula to each Annual Conference. Each Annual Conference, using its own approved formula, apportions these fund requests along with conference administrative and benevolence fund requests to local churches.

archives. Public and historical records of local churches, Annual Conferences, and the denomination. Such materials include minutes, journals of proceedings, reports, and other records. Each local church, Annual Conference, and agency of the denomination is requested to properly maintain and preserve its records and archival materials.

See also *Archives and History, General Commission on.*

Archives and History, General Commission on. The agency established by the General Conference to gather, preserve, hold title to, and disseminate materials on the history of The United Methodist Church and its antecedents.

It maintains archives and a library in which the historical records and materials are kept. Its offices and archives are located at Drew University, Madison, New Jersey.

area, episcopal. The Annual Conference or Conferences to which a bishop is assigned by the Jurisdictional Conference. The bishop lives within the bounds of the episcopal area and presides over the work of the one or more Annual Conferences in the area.

The bishop is responsible for the churches in the episcopal area, including the appointment of ministers.

See also *bishop.*

Articles of Religion. The series of twenty-five doctrinal statements considered part of the doctrinal standards of The United Methodist Church. The original list of thirty-nine was first adopted by the Church of England in 1563. John Wesley abridged this list to twenty-four (editing out much of their Calvinist emphasis).

He sent them to America as an appendix to his proposed prayerbook for the American Methodists. The 1784 Christmas Conference added what is now Article 23. In 1808 the General Conference of The Methodist Episcopal Church passed the first Restrictive Rule, which states that the General Conference may not in any way change the Articles of Religion. They remain unchanged to this day and have been printed without change in every edition of *The Book of Discipline.*

See also *Restrictive Rules, the.*

Asbury, Francis. The dominant figure in the formation and growth of The Methodist Episcopal Church in the United States. Asbury (1745–1816) was born in

Birmingham, England, and in his early adult life became a lay preacher in England. Responding to John Wesley's call for a preacher to go to America, he arrived in 1771. Wesley designated Asbury a "General Superintendent" of what was to be the first independent Methodist denomination. At the 1784 Christmas Conference, Asbury was unanimously elected and consecrated as a general superintendent, and he immediately began to travel throughout the church. In 1788 the words "general superintendent" were supplanted by the word "bishop," to the consternation of Wesley.

Francis Asbury was the guiding hand in the development of the structure and polity of the new denomination.

Ash Wednesday. The first day of Lent. It marks the beginning of a period of reflection and penance. In the Bible, sprinkling oneself with ashes was traditionally a sign of one's sorrow for having committed sins. In the Christian tradition, Ash Wednesday also marked the beginning of preparation for the understanding of the death and resurrection of Christ. The particular symbolism of ashes for this day comes from a practice in the Roman Catholic churches in which the ashes from the palms used in the preceding year's Palm Sunday celebration are blessed. With these ashes, the priest on the first day of Lent marks a cross on the forehead of each worshiper. This practice has become a part of Ash Wednesday services in many United Methodist churches.

See also *Lent*.

Asian American Federation.

See *National Federation of Asian American United Methodists*.

33

associate member of a local church (lay). A lay member of another denomination, residing away from home for an extended period, who attends a United Methodist church may be enrolled as an associate member. The associate member may hold office, except for those that would place him or her on the Administrative Board or Council. This person is still considered a member of the home church.

associate member of an Annual Conference (ministerial). Ministerial members of the Annual Conference, to be appointed by the bishops to pastorates in local churches or to other areas of service.

Associate members have not met all the requirements for full ministerial membership in the Annual Conference. They are eligible for ordination as deacons, but not as elders.

They may serve as members of Annual Conference boards and agencies. They may vote on all matters coming before the Annual Conference with the exception of constitutional amendments, election of delegates to General and Jurisdictional Conferences, and matters related to ordination and conference relations of ministers.

Autonomous Methodist Church. A self-governing Methodist church outside the United States. Historically, its establishment has been assisted by The United Methodist Church or one of its predecessor bodies (The Evangelical United Brethren Church or The Methodist Church). Autonomous Methodist churches may or may not have entered into the Act of Covenanting with The United Methodist Church.

See also *Act of Covenanting.*

**B**

Baptism, Sacrament of. One of the two sacraments recognized by The United Methodist Church and most Protestant denominations. Baptism is the sacrament by which the individual is received into the Christian faith through the symbol of water baptism. The individual comes to baptism through the profession of faith in Jesus Christ as Lord and Savior and the repentance of past sins. Through baptism one enters into the Baptismal Covenant. It is God's word to Christians, accepting them through grace, and the Christian's word to God, promising to respond in faith and love. Through the vows affirmed at baptism, the individual enters into the larger fellowship of all believing Christians, not just into the denomination called United Methodist. Because baptism marks entrance into the community of faith, for United Methodists baptism takes place in the presence of the congregation as an integral part of a service of worship.

In The United Methodist Church baptism may be performed by immersion, pouring, or sprinkling. In recent years, baptism by sprinkling (the minister dips his or her hand in water and then places it on the person being baptized) has been the most common method.

baptismal covenant. The covenant representing God's word of grace to Christians and their response to God of love and faith. The individual's entrance into this covenant is symbolized by the Sacrament of Baptism and reception into the membership of the denomination.

In recent years the development in United Methodism of the understanding of Christian life as a covenant with God has been given heightened emphasis. One of the consequences of this is that the title "The Baptismal Covenant" is now applied to the services of baptism, confirmation, and reaffirmation of faith. These services are found under this title in the front portion of *The United Methodist Hymnal.*

baptismal font.
See *font, baptismal.*

benediction. A traditional close to the worship services with a word of blessing. Literally, benediction means "a good saying or word." Spoken by the pastor and addressed to the congregation, it is used to dismiss the congregation at the end of worship.

benevolences. The term used in The United Methodist Church to describe monetary gifts to causes carrying out the mission and program of the denomination. These funds are distinguished from those which provide for the administration of the church organization, such as administrative expenditures and salaries at the local church, the Annual Conference, and denominational levels. In the Annual

Conference they are called Conference Benevolences. In the general church they are called World Service Benevolences.

bequests. Contributions to the local church, the Annual Conference, or the general agencies, which come from donors through specifically designated gifts or provisions in a will.

Bible. The collection of books of the Old and New Testaments which are considered authoritative as Scripture. A portion of "Our Theological Task" in *The Book of Discipline* includes the following statements as approved by the 1988 General Conference.

"The Bible is sacred canon for Christian people, formally acknowledged as such by historic ecumenical councils of the Church. Our [United Methodist] doctrinal standards identify as canonical thirty-nine books of the Old Testament and the twenty-seven books of the New Testament.

"Our standards affirm the Bible as the source of all that is 'necessary' and 'sufficient' unto salvation (Articles of Religion) and 'is to be received through the Holy Spirit as the true rule and guide for faith and practice' (Confession of Faith).

"We properly read Scripture within the believing community, informed by the tradition of that community. We interpret individual texts in light of their place in the Bible as a whole."

See also *Articles of Religion; canon.*

bishop. An elder (ordained minister) who has been elected to the office of bishop by the lay and ministerial delegates of a Jurisdictional or Central Conference. Unlike the Roman Catholic, Anglican, and Orthodox traditions, The United Methodist Church considers the episcopacy an "office" and not a third order of ministry (along with deacon and elder). A United Methodist bishop is consecrated for the office of bishop by other United Methodist bishops. A bishop serves as a general superintendent of the denomination. As such, individually and collectively bishops give general oversight to the temporal and spiritual interests of the entire denomination. It is a responsibility of the bishops to see that the rules, regulations, and responsibilities developed by the General Conference are understood and effectively carried out. The Greek word for bishop is *episcopos*, which is the root word for episcopal.

Black Methodists for Church Renewal (BMCR).

A caucus organized to hold the concerns and issues of Black United Methodists before The United Methodist Church. Black Methodists for Church Renewal is one of four caucuses which represent and advocate for racial and ethnic groups within the denomination.

See also *caucus*.

blessing.

The asking for or the pronouncement of God's favor. Though often said by a minister, it can be said by anyone. A common form of blessing is the prayer said at meals in thanksgiving for the food and the asking of God's favor on those who partake.

board.

At the general level of the denomination, a continuing body created by the General Conference to carry out certain functions of program, administration, and service. Four general boards are related to program: Church and Society, Discipleship, Global

Ministries, and Higher Education and Ministry. Two general boards perform service functions: Pensions and Publication. The chief staff officer of a general board is a general secretary.

At the Annual Conference level there are counterpart agencies (with the exception of Publication), which carry program and service activities in these same areas. Annual Conference and general boards provide guidance and resources for local church work areas in these areas of program and service.

Board, Administrative.

See *Administrative Board.*

Board of Church and Society, General.

See *Church and Society, General Board of.*

Board of Church Location and Building, district.

Consists of the district superintendent and a minimum of six and a maximum of nine lay and ministerial members. The board is to investigate and approve all local church and parsonage building sites, approve the construction, purchase, and remodeling plans of local churches and parsonages, and approve the sale, transfer, lease, or mortgage of district property.

Board of Diaconal Ministry, Annual Conference.

See *Diaconal Ministry, Annual Conference Board of.*

Board of Discipleship, General.

See *Discipleship, General Board of.*

Board of Global Ministries, General.

See *Global Ministries, General Board of.*

Board of Higher Education and Ministry, General.

See *Higher Education and Ministry, General Board of.*

Board of Pensions, General.

See *Pensions, General Board of.*

Board of Publication, General.

See *United Methodist Publishing House, The.*

Board of Stewards, district.

The organization responsible for assigning apportionments to local churches when an Annual Conference makes apportionments to the districts only (and not directly to local churches). The district Board of Stewards receives the apportionment to the district, determines the formula to be used, and makes apportionments to local churches or pastoral charges. Each pastoral charge elects one person to serve on the district Board of Stewards. The district superintendent is the chairperson.

The word *steward* has largely disappeared as a title for an official position in the United Methodist tradition. Formerly, members of the Official Board (now called the Administrative Board) were called stewards.

Board of Trustees, Annual Conference.

See *Trustees, Annual Conference Board of.*

Board of Trustees, local church.

See *Trustees, local church Board of.*

Book of Discipline, The.

See *Discipline, The Book of.*

Book of Resolutions, The.
See *Resolutions, The Book of.*

Book of Worship, The.
See *Worship, The Book of.*

boundaries. The geographical limits of the various conferences and districts in The United Methodist Church.

The boundaries of the Jurisdictional Conferences are stated in The Constitution and may be changed only by amendment by action of the General Conference. Similarly the boundaries of the Central Conferences may be changed only by action of the General Conference.

Changes in the number, names, and boundaries of Annual Conferences may be done only by the appropriate Jurisdictional or Central Conference.

Each Annual Conference determines the number of districts it will have. The bishop, in consultation with the district superintendents, has the right to establish the boundaries for the districts.

boycott. A concerted effort to abstain from the purchase or use of products or services provided by a targeted firm, government, or other agency. *The Book of Resolutions* contains a set of guidelines for initiating or joining a boycott. These guidelines are recommended for the General Conference, Annual Conferences, districts, or local churches when they are contemplating a boycott. The word *boycott* derives from Charles Boycott, a land agent in Ireland who was ostracized in 1880 for refusing to reduce rents.

bread. One of the elements of the Service of the Lord's Supper. The bread may be leavened (with yeast) or unleavened (without yeast). The custom varies among individual United Methodist churches about whether wafers, cubes, or loaves are used in the service. All are acceptable. The bread in the service assists us to remember Christ as the bread of life. It is also the symbol of the body of Christ broken for the redemption of the world.

C

Cabinet. The organization in an Annual Conference whose membership consists of the resident bishop and the district superintendents. The Cabinet provides oversight and direction for the work of the Annual Conference, districts, and local churches. The Cabinet works as a unit on developing the appointments for the ministerial members, which are made or fixed by the bishop.

calendar, Christian. Six distinct periods of Christian observances. Each focuses upon a different aspect of the Christian experience and tradition. These periods or seasons do not necessarily occur on the same dates from year to year, but are related to the dates of the two principal Christian celebrations of Christmas and Easter. (1) *Advent* begins four Sundays before Christmas. (2) The *Christmas Season* includes the twelve days from sunset Christmas Eve (December 24) through Epiphany (January 6). (3) The *Season After Epiphany* begins January 7 and lasts until Ash Wednesday. (4) *Lent* begins on Ash Wednesday and lasts until Easter. The exact dates of Lent depend on the date for Easter Sunday. (5) *Easter* is the first Sunday after the first full moon after

March 21. Because the date for Easter moves between March 22 and April 25, the length of the Season After Epiphany and the Season After Pentecost varies. The Easter Season is fifty days long and goes through the Day of Pentecost. (6) The *Season After Pentecost* begins immediately after Pentecost Sunday and continues until the beginning of Advent.

candidacy for ministry. The series of steps required of every person seeking to enter into the ordained or diaconal ministry of The United Methodist Church. These steps are outlined in detail in *The Book of Discipline* and are administered by the Annual Conference Board of Ordained Ministry or Board of Diaconal Ministry. The steps involve an examination of the candidate in relation to the personal, spiritual, academic, and professional qualifications of the person for ministry.

canon. The books of the Bible recognized as having authority as Scripture and as being accepted for use. The word *canon* comes from the Greek word meaning ruler or measuring rod. Thus, books accepted as Scripture are considered canonical, a demand that they meet the measure or standard. The list of books acceptable as Jewish scripture (those books Christians have come to call the Old Testament) was established by Jewish rabbis before the time of Jesus. This is the list most Protestants accept and use today. The list of New Testament books stabilized within the first three centuries of the Christian church.

canticle. A song using texts from the Scriptures (generally other than the Psalms) or traditional Christian texts. Canticles are often sung by the congregation following the reading of a Scripture lesson.

cassock. A long gown or vestment, usually black in color, traditionally worn by Roman Catholic and Anglican clergy. It is rarely worn by United Methodist ministers. In some United Methodist churches, however, a form of the cassock is worn by acolytes under their surplice. Some choirs also have a cassock-like vestment, which is worn under a surplice.

See also *surplice.*

CASSOCK

catholic. Derived from a Greek word meaning universal. When spelled with a capital "C" in current usage, Catholic has come to be accepted as a shortened reference to the Roman Catholic Church or to one of its members. When spelled with the lower case "c," catholic means universal. The use in the Apostles' Creed in the phrase "the holy catholic church" means the entire body of Christian believers or the church universal.

caucus. A group of persons who have joined together to devise policies and positions appropriate to the concerns of the group and who jointly act to advocate for that group and to influence larger entities to respond to their requests and respond to their issues. In The United Methodist Church, a number of caucuses have been formed both denomination-wide and in the Annual Conference. These are unofficial bodies in that they have not been established through action by the General Conference or the Annual Conference and are not accountable to those bodies. Among the oldest and most prominent of the caucuses are the four which have formed to relate to the issues and concerns of four racial and ethnic groups in America: Black Methodists for Church Renewal (BMCR), Methodists Associated Representing the Cause of Hispanic Americans (MARCHA), Native American International Caucus (NAIC), and National Federation of Asian American United Methodists (NFAAUM).

Central Conference. The organizational structure established for the work of The United Methodist Church in countries other than the United States of America. The number and boundaries of the Central Conferences are determined by the General Conference. Each Central Conference oversees the work of Annual Conferences, Provisional Annual Conferences, and Mission Conferences within its boundaries. Central Conferences function in much the same way as the Jurisdictional Conferences function in the United States.

certification, leadership. The procedure by which persons in The United Methodist Church meet

46

specific standards for designated leadership roles such as Christian education laboratory leader, mission study leader, seminar teacher, lay speaker, and others. Each leadership responsibility has its own set of requirements and procedures.

certification, professional. The procedure by which persons in The United Methodist Church who are professionally employed in the church may meet personal, denominational, academic, and service requirements of various agencies of the denomination for certification in their specific professional field. Upon certification, these persons may serve as ministers, directors, and associates in fields such as Christian education, music, evangelism, church business administration, communication, and others.

certified lay speaker. A lay person who has completed the required training courses in lay speaking and has been approved by a district or Annual Conference Committee on Lay Speaking. When certified, the lay speaker may conduct services of worship, preach, and lead study sessions as requested by pastors of local churches or by the district superintendent.

chalice. The container or vessel used to hold the wine in the Sacrament of the Lord's Supper or Holy Communion. The chalice is also referred to as the "Cup," which is the word used in the Service of Word and Table (The Lord's Supper). Although chalices are often made of silver, they may be fashioned from any appropriate material.

chancel. Historically, that portion of the church or sanctuary which was reserved for the clergy. Often it was set apart from the rest of the church by lattices or crossbars. The Latin word for this screen is *cancelli,* from which chancel is derived.

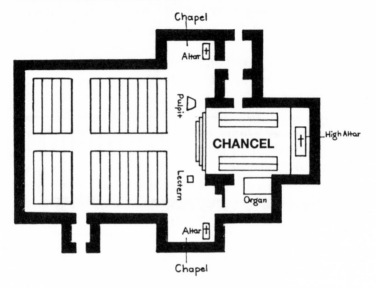

In modern usage the word *chancel* refers to the area around the Lord's table or communion table. In United Methodist churches the chancel is generally raised and includes the area in which the communion table, pulpit, and lectern are found. The organ console and choir seating also are often in this area. Usually the chancel is set apart from the remainder of the room by a low railing.

See also *chancel railing or rail.*

chancel railing or rail. The low railing which in many United Methodist churches separates the chancel from the remainder of the worship sanctuary or room.

Generally it is constructed in such a way as to include a kneeling bench along its entire length. It is common practice in many United Methodist churches for the worshipers to come forward and kneel at the chancel railing to receive Holy Communion. The chancel railing

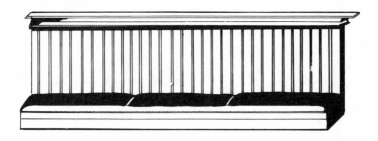

CHANCEL RAILING

is also sometimes referred to as the altar. When persons are invited to come forward to the altar for prayer or special observances, it is to the chancel railing, not the communion table, that they come.

chant. A method of singing parts of a worship service such as the Psalms, canticles, litanies, or other portions of the service with or without the aid of instrumental music. Chants have no set number of syllables per note and many have no set meter.

chapel. Used in United Methodist churches to refer to a room set aside for worship that is other than the main sanctuary or worship center. Chapel is also used to refer to a worship setting in a college, seminary, hospital, or other institution. Only rarely in the United States is chapel used to refer to a local church.

chapel (Wesley's use of). The term used by John Wesley for consecrated buildings used for worship by his Methodist followers. In England in the time of John Wesley, the use of the word *church* was limited to those buildings which had been formally consecrated as places of worship by the Church of England. Wesley used the term *preaching-houses* for the places where his followers gathered. After Wesley's death the term *chapel* was increasingly used in British Methodism to refer to the Methodist places of worship. This is still the practice.

charge, pastoral. One or more local churches organized according to *The Book of Discipline*. The pastoral charge is governed by a Charge Conference. An ordained minister or local pastor is appointed by the bishop to be the pastor in charge.

Charge Conference. The basic governing body of a United Methodist pastoral charge composed of all members of the Administrative Board or Administrative Council. The Charge Conference must meet at least once a year. The district superintendent presides or designates another ordained minister to do so. The Charge Conference serves as the connecting link between the local church and the Annual Conference and general church, and directs the work of the pastoral charge according to the policies and plans of *The Book of Discipline*. Among its responsibilities, the Charge Conference reviews and evaluates the mission and ministry of the church, receives reports, adopts objectives and goals, elects the members of the Administrative Board or Council and other officers, sets the salary of the pastor and other staff, and recommends to the district Committee on Ordained Ministry candidates for the ordained ministry.

charges against a minister or lay member.

The initial step in the process of beginning an investigation or trial of a lay member or minister. The United Methodist Church has a detailed process for the investigations, trials, and appeals of ordained ministers, local pastors, diaconal ministers, and lay persons. *The Book of Discipline* lists those offenses for which charges can be made and the procedures for making them. When charges are made, the facts relating to the charges must also be presented. Upon receipt of the charges, steps are begun for the investigation of the charges and, if needed, for a trial.

Children's Age-Level Council, local church.

The group established when needed in a local United Methodist church to facilitate the planning and implementation of the entire ministry of the congregation to children. The membership of the Children's Age-Level Council is elected by the Council on Ministries or the Administrative Council. The membership may consist of representative teachers and leaders of children's activities, representative parents, and representatives of the various local church work areas.

choir. An organized group of singers in the local church who participate regularly in the worship services. The choir serves both to lead the congregation in its singing and to present special anthems.

The term *choir* (or *choir loft*) is also used to designate that part of the sanctuary set aside for the seating of the singers.

Christ candle. The large white candle used on Christmas Eve or on Christmas Day or both. The Christ candle is often the candle located in the center of an Advent wreath.

Christian Advocate, The.
See *Advocate, The Christian.*

Christian Education Sunday. A special Sunday authorized by General Conference to be observed without a churchwide offering. Christian Education Sunday is to be observed on a date determined by each Annual Conference. This special Sunday calls United Methodists to be open to growth and learning as disciples of Jesus Christ. If it so desires, an Annual Conference may have an offering taken as a part of the observance with the proceeds to be used for the work of Christian education within the Annual Conference.

Christian Social Action. A magazine published by the General Board of Church and Society that focuses on the principal social issues and concerns facing The United Methodist Church and the United States of America. The magazine was formerly called *engage/social action.*

Christian Unity and Interreligious Concerns, General Commission on. The commission established by the General Conference to advocate

for and work toward Christian unity in every aspect of the life of The United Methodist Church. It works to enable ecumenical and interreligious understanding and experience among all United Methodists.

The General Commission is at the forefront of ecumenical activity on behalf of the denomination. Its offices are in New York City. *The Book of Discipline* also provides that there shall be a Commission on Christian Unity and Interreligious Concerns in each Annual Conference to address these same concerns.

Christian Unity and Interreligious Concerns, local church work area on.
The work area in each local church that addresses the issues related to Christian unity and interreligious concerns. It is designed to encourage the local church in awareness and understanding of ecumenism and includes work in councils of churches and interfaith councils.

Christmas.
The day on which Christians celebrate the birth of Jesus Christ. Although the actual day of the year of the birth is not known, most Christians in the Western world celebrate the birth on December 25. The word *Christmas* comes from the early English phrase *Christes Masse*, which means Christ's Mass. The day is also commemorated as the Feast of the Nativity.

Christmas Conference.
The name given to the conference at which The Methodist Episcopal Church in America was formally organized. The conference began on December 24, 1784, and lasted until January 2 or 3, 1785, at the Lovely Lane Chapel in Baltimore, Maryland. Because of meeting through the Christmas period, the conference has traditionally been called the Christmas Conference. It was at this conference

that John Wesley's instructions for the new church were received and approved. Thomas Coke was received as a general superintendent. Francis Asbury, designated a general superintendent by Wesley, was elected to the office by the ministers present and consecrated. Ministers were ordained, and ministerial appointments to churches and circuits were made. The initial policies for the new church were chosen. The founding date of 1784 for The United Methodist Church comes from this meeting of the Christmas Conference.

Christmas Season. The second of six seasons in the Christian calendar. The Christmas Season begins at sunset Christmas Eve and lasts, in United Methodist usage, through Epiphany (January 6). The liturgical color for the Christmas Season is white.

church, local. The congregation of persons who have joined together as Christians and as United Methodists to carry forward the message of Christ and to be of witness and service to the world. It is the fellowship of persons who have professed their belief in Christ, have been baptized, and who have taken the vows of membership of The United Methodist Church. The local church is the context for the hearing of the Word of God and for the receiving of the Sacraments. The local church is organized in accordance with and subject to the provisions of *The Book of Discipline.* The local church is to reach out in the name of Christ to bring persons into its fellowship, to nurture the members in their faith, and to witness to and serve the community, both local and global.

Church and Society, General Board of. The agency, established by the General Conference, that challenges United Methodists to work, through their local church and communities, in areas of important social concern. This board provides resources to assist in the analysis of these social issues, and it encourages Christian lines of action that assist people to move toward a world of peace and justice. Prime responsibilities include working for the implementation of the Social Principles and other policy statements on social concerns of the General Conference, and developing resources to inform, motivate, and train United Methodists on issues of social justice in the society. The Board's offices are located in Washington, D.C. *The Book of Discipline* also provides that there shall be a Board of Church and Society in each Annual Conference to address these same purposes and issues.

Church and Society, local church work area on. The work area in each local church whose task it is to keep the Council on Ministries or the Administrative Council aware of the need for study and action in areas of peace, justice, and social issues. The work area is to recommend to the Council on Ministries or Administrative Council study and action plans related to issues of social concern.

Church Conference. The convening of the Charge Conference as a meeting in which all members of a local United Methodist church are invited to attend and are extended the privilege of vote. A Church Conference is called to have the broad participation of the members of the congregation. The Church Conference may be authorized by the district superintendent.

Church of England, The. Established during the reign of Henry VIII of England in the course of his controversy with the Roman Catholic Church over his divorce from Catherine of Aragon. At Henry's direction, the church in England declared it no longer accepted the Roman pope as its head and became independent of the Roman Catholic Church. Subsequently, the Church of England became the established and dominant religious body of England. With the spread of the British colonies, missionaries, and culture throughout the world, many independent churches were formed which traced their identity and forms of worship to the Church of England. These have formed a worldwide association of communions or churches and regard the Archbishop of Canterbury as their spiritual leader. United Methodism traces its roots back to the Church of England through John and Charles Wesley, who were educated in Church of England institutions and who were ordained ministers of the Church of England their entire adult lives.

Church of the United Brethren in Christ, The. One of the predecessor denominations of The United Methodist Church. The church was formally organized in September of 1800 following a number of years of less formal fellowship among lay persons and ministers. The church began as a movement among German-speaking lay people who were influenced by the preaching of Philip Otterbein. He later came into close association with a German Mennonite, Martin Boehm. At the time of its organizing conference in 1800, both Otterbein and Boehm were elected the first bishops. It initially served the German immigrants in Maryland, Pennsylvania, and Virginia. As this population group moved west so did the church, so that it soon had considerable strength in Ohio, Indiana, and Illinois. It held its first delegated General Conference in 1815 and approved a Discipline, a Confession of Faith, and the basic form for its church government. In 1946, The Church of the United Brethren in Christ merged with the Evangelical Church to form The Evangelical United Brethren Church. This in turn merged with The Methodist Church in 1968 to form The United Methodist Church.

church school. The program of the local church for instructing and guiding its entire membership and constituency in Christian faith and living. Church school settings include the Sunday church school, youth groups, Bible study groups, and all other continuing and short-term classes and learning groups for persons of all ages.

church trials and trial procedures. The body of regulations enacted by the General Conference to make provision for and guide the conduct of trials and appeals for United Methodist ministers and lay persons. Trials of ministers and lay persons may be held in The United Methodist Church in relation to certain specified chargeable offenses. Once the charges have been properly filed and an investigation has taken place, a trial may be called if deemed necessary. *The Book of Discipline* outlines the procedures for setting up and conducting a trial. Provisions are also established for making appeals to the next higher level of judicial trial and hearing.

church year.
See *calendar, Christian.*

cincture. A rope or band placed around the waist of a cassock or an alb. Generally, it is the same color as the garment over which it is worn, but it may be the color of the season.

CINCTURE ——————

circuit. Two or more local churches joined together for pastoral supervision. The churches on a circuit constitute one pastoral charge. When a pastoral charge consists of only one local church, it is called a station.

See also *charge, pastoral.*

circuit rider. A term of historic usage in American Methodism. From the earliest years of the denomination, pastors were appointed to serve a large number of local churches and preaching places located within a large geographic area. These ministers traveled regularly throughout their assigned areas and came to be known as circuit riders.

Circuit Rider. A monthly magazine for United Methodist clergy published by The United Methodist Publishing House.

clergy. In United Methodism, only those who have been ordained as deacons or elders. These persons are also ministerial members of an Annual Conference. The word *clergy* comes from the Latin *clericus,* meaning priest.

Cokesbury. The word was formed by combining Coke and Asbury, the names of the first two general superintendents of The Methodist Episcopal Church in America. The primary use of the word *Cokesbury* today is that of The United Methodist Publishing House as the name for its retail bookstores and mail order service. Prior to 1939 Cokesbury Press was the trade name of the publishing house of The Methodist Episcopal Church, South. At union in 1939, the names of the publishing houses were combined to form Abingdon-Cokesbury. Subsequently, the name Abingdon was used as the trade name for the publishing house and Cokesbury for the bookstores.

The name Cokesbury has a long history in American Methodism. In 1787 Cokesbury College opened in Abingdon, Maryland. The college continued until 1795 when a fire destroyed the building. It then moved to Baltimore and in 1796 its building was again destroyed. No further attempts were made to rebuild the college.

collect. ('käl-ikt, -,ekt) A short prayer with a very precise form. It contains an address to God referring to some attribute of God, a petition relating to that attribute, a reference to the desired result of the petition, and closing words stating that the prayer is through Jesus Christ.

College of Bishops.

All bishops assigned to or elected by a Jurisdictional or Central Conference. A College of Bishops includes both active and retired bishops. The retired bishops have the right to speak but not to vote. The College annually elects a president and carries out responsibilities assigned to it by the Council of Bishops or *The Book of Discipline.*

colors, liturgical.

The colors symbolizing the days and seasons of the Christian year, used for stoles and other vestments, altar cloths and other paraments, and church decorations. The liturgical colors are as follows: Advent, purple; Christmas, white; Season After Epiphany, white for the first and last Sundays and green at other times; Lent, purple; Easter, white until the Day of Pentecost and red on that day; Season After Pentecost, white for the first and last Sundays and for All Saints Day and green at other times.

commission. At the general level of the denomination, a continuing body created by the General Conference to accomplish a specific task. From time to time the General Conference will establish study commissions for a limited period of time to prepare reports and recommendations for consideration by the General Conference. It has also established five permanent general commissions: Archives and History, Christian

Unity and Interreligious Concerns, Communication, Religion and Race, and Status and Role of Women. The chief staff officer of a permanent commission is a general secretary.

In the Annual Conferences there are counterpart commissions, which have programs and responsibilities in the same areas as those of the national commissions. Annual Conference and general commissions provide guidance and resources for local church work areas.

Commission on Archives and History, General.
See *Archives and History, General Commission on.*

Commission on Christian Unity and Interreligious Concerns.
See *Christian Unity and Interreligious Concerns, General Commission on.*

Commission on Communication, General.
See *United Methodist Communications.*

Commission on Pan-Methodist Cooperation.
The commission developed jointly by The United Methodist Church, The African Methodist Episcopal Church, The African Methodist Episcopal Zion Church, and The Christian Methodist Episcopal Church. The Commission for Pan-Methodist cooperation was developed out of the recognition of the historical relationships and the shared traditions of these denominations. The Commission is to plan for and devise activities that foster meaningful cooperation among the four denominations.

Commission on Religion and Race, General.

See *Religion and Race, General Commission on.*

Commission on the Status and Role of Women, General.

See *Status and Role of Women, General Commission on the.*

Committal, Service of. The ritual used at the grave site for the burial of the dead. The pastor presides at the Service of Committal. The service is primarily for burial in the ground, but it can be adapted in the instances of cremation or burial above ground or at sea.

committee. A group, either temporary or permanent, at any level in the denomination, created to carry out certain functions of mission, study, oversight, administration, or review. A committee is amenable to the parent body which establishes it.

communion, a denomination. The use of the word to refer to a denomination as a whole. In this sense, communion means a body of Christians who share a set of beliefs, rituals, customs, and government. For example, The United Methodist Church is a communion. The National Council of Churches of Christ is often referred to as an organization of Christian communions.

Communion, Holy.

See *Lord's Supper, Sacrament of the.*

communion stewards. Persons elected by the Charge Conference to be responsible for the prepara-

tion of the bread, wine, and the communion ware for use in the Sacrament of the Lord's Supper.

concordat. The formal agreement between the General Conference of The United Methodist Church and a similar body of an autonomous Methodist church or a united church. A concordat agreement provides for a limited number from each church to be members of the highest legislative body of the other. The agreement also implies a commitment to mutual support and cooperation. The United Methodist Church has entered into concordat agreements with The Methodist Church of Great Britain, The Methodist Church in the Caribbean and the Americas, and The Methodist Church of Mexico.

Conference, Annual.
See *Annual Conference.*

Conference, Central.
See *Central Conference.*

Conference, Charge.
See *Charge Conference.*

Conference, Church.
See *Church Conference.*

Conference, District.
See *District Conference.*

Conference, General.
See *General Conference.*

Conference, Jurisdictional.
See *Jurisdictional Conference.*

Conference, Missionary.
See *Missionary Conference.*

Conference, Provisional Annual.
See *Provisional Annual Conference.*

Conference benevolences. The Annual Conference allocations and expenditures directly associated with the program, mission, and benevolence causes of Annual Conference program agencies and institutions. Administrative expenses directly related to the program, mission, and benevolent causes of Conference program agencies, including the expenses of the Annual Conference Council on Ministries, are often included in the Conference benevolence budget. The term *Conference benevolences* does not include allocations and expenditures for other Conference agencies and offices whose work is primarily administrative. Also not included are funds for clergy support such as pensions and health care.

Conference claimants. Persons who have a claim upon the Annual Conference retirement or pension funds. Conference claimants include retired ministers, surviving spouses of ministers, and dependent children of deceased ministers.

Conference Journal. The annual volume in which each Annual Conference publishes the reports and records of its activities for the year. Each Annual Conference is required to keep an exact record of its proceedings according to instructions and forms supplied by the

General, Jurisdictional, and Central Conferences. The journal should include the following: (1) a list of the officers of the Annual Conference, (2) names and addresses of the Conference lay and clergy members and the members of all Conference organizations, (3) a record of the daily proceedings of the Annual Conference sessions, (4) answers to the Disciplinary questions, (5) a listing of all ministerial appointments, (6) reports ordered by the Conference, (7) memoirs and roll of the deceased clergy members, (8) service records of ministers, (9) a listing of diaconal ministers, deaconesses, and missionaries of the Conference, and (10) statistics for each local church.

The Journal of the General Conference consists of *The Daily Christian Advocate, Advance Edition* and *The Daily Christian Advocate.* These include the listing of delegates, the listing of petitions received, the calendar items containing the results of legislative committee action, and the transcript of the daily proceedings. *The United Methodist Hymnal* approved by the 1988 General Conference also is a part of the official record of the 1988 General Conference.

Each Jurisdictional and Central Conference is also to keep an official journal of its proceedings.

Confession of Faith, the. A statement devised by The Evangelical United Brethren Church. The 1946 Discipline of the then newly formed Evangelical United Brethren Church contained both the amended Articles of Religion of The Evangelical Association and the Confession of Faith of The Church of the United Brethren in Christ. In 1958 the General Conference of The Evangelical United Brethren Church authorized its bishops to prepare a new Confession of Faith.

The new Confession, with sixteen articles, was presented to the General Conference of 1962 and was

65

adopted without amendment. This Confession of Faith replaced both the former Articles of Religion and Confession. At the time of the union in 1968 with The Methodist Church, the Confession of Faith was included as one of the historic doctrinal statements of The United Methodist Church. It appears in *The Book of Discipline* in the section "Our Doctrinal Standards and General Rules." Like the Articles of Religion and the General Rules of the former Methodist Church, the Confession of Faith is protected by the Restrictive Rules of the Constitution. This means that these doctrinal standards may not be changed by the General Conference.

See also *Restrictive Rules, the.*

confirmation. The act by which persons who were baptized as infants or young children (or, because of other special circumstances, could not make the baptismal vows themselves) make their first public statement of their declaration or profession of faith. In this sense they confirm their faith.

Confirmation is performed in preparation for reception into full membership in The United Methodist Church. Persons who declared their faith in Christ for themselves at their baptism are not confirmed inasmuch as they previously made their profession of faith when baptized.

Connection, the. The term frequently used to refer to the entire organization of The United Methodist Church. The use of "connection" originated in Great Britain. John Wesley did not refer to his followers as "members" of his movement, since he believed that they should remain members of the Church of England. Rather he referred to his preachers as being "in connection with him." In the first years of The Methodist Episcopal Church in America, the new church was often referred to as "the Connection." The Constitution of The United Methodist Church states: "The General Conference shall have full legislative power over all matters distinctively connectional."

Connection means that local churches and Annual Conferences are in a covenant, connected relationship with each other. Local churches are not independent entities. Within The United Methodist Church there are numerous sets of mutual rights and obligations, which connect the local church, the Annual Conference, and the General Conference in order to best serve the interests of all and to promote the work of Christian ministry.

connectional principle, the. The statement first approved by the 1988 General Conference which describes the concept of "the connection" as an integral part of United Methodism. The text of the connectional principle is included in *The Book of Discipline* as follows:

The United Methodist connectional principle, born out of our historical tradition, many biblical roots, and accepted theological ideas, is the basic form of our polity, the way in which we carry out God's mission as a people.

It is in essence a network of interdependent relationships among persons and groups throughout the life of the whole denomination.

It declares that our identity is in our wholeness together in Christ, that each part is vital to the whole, that our mission is more effectively carried out by a connectional life which incorporates Wesleyan zeal into the life of the people.

consecration of a person. The act in United Methodism of setting aside a person for a specific office or ministry within the denomination. Consecration for United Methodists is not a form of ordination or the induction of a person into a new and distinct order. Bishops are consecrated for their office. Diaconal ministers are also consecrated.

consecration of church property. The service in which a United Methodist church building, parsonage, or other church property is formally set aside to enhance the life and mission of the Christian faith.

Constituency Roll. The record each local United Methodist church is to maintain which contains a list of the names and addresses of those persons who are constituents of the congregation.

constituent. A person who is related to a local United Methodist church in some way but who is *not* a member. Constituents include unbaptized children, dedicated children, persons enrolled in the church school, persons who are preparatory members and who have reached age nineteen without being received into full membership, and other non-members for whom the church has pastoral responsibility.

Constitution, the. The fundamental constituting and legal document of The United Methodist Church. The Constitution was approved as part of the Plan of Union for the merger of The Evangelical United Brethren Church and The Methodist Church in 1968. It establishes the basic outline for the organization of the denomination as well as establishing the office and role of the bishop. The Constitution establishes the

Judicial Council as the body to rule on matters of church law as passed by the General Conference. The Constitution may only be amended by a two-thirds majority of the General Conference *and* a two-thirds affirmative vote of the aggregate number of members of all Annual Conferences. The Constitution is printed in *The Book of Discipline.*

See also *Judicial Council; Restrictive Rules, the.*

consultation. The process by which the bishop or the district superintendent confers with a minister and with the local church Committee on Pastor-Parish Relations concerning the appointment of a pastor to the local church. This process of consultation is required by *The Book of Discipline,* which contains a description of the consultation procedures to be followed.

Consultation on Church Union. An ecumenical organization of Protestant denominations focusing on discussions leading to shared understandings of polity, ritual, and ordination. The United Methodist Church has been a member of the Consultation on Church Union (COCU) from its very beginning.

conversion. The act of a person's being born spiritually into the Kingdom of God. Through conversion the individual recognizes Jesus Christ as Lord and Savior and accepts the doctrines of Christianity as the guide for future living. The formal entrance of the new convert into the Christian community is through the Sacrament of Baptism.

cooperative parish. Two or more pastoral charges, joined together to coordinate program and organization to fulfill their ministry. Cooperative parishes are conceived because of particular needs or geographic location of the local churches involved. The pastoral charges join together in order to more fully make use of the resources and to improve the ministry to all of the people of a general geographic area. The pastors of the pastoral charges often work together in a team relationship in the cooperative parish.

council. A continuing body created by the General Conference or established by the Constitution charged with review or oversight responsibility over an aspect of the life and work of The United Methodist Church. The two councils established by the Constitution are the Council of Bishops and the Judicial Council. The two established by the General Conference are the General Council on Finance and Administration and the General Council on Ministries.

Councils on the Annual Conference, district, and local church levels are governing bodies with those powers and functions given to them by *The Book of Discipline* or by the proper authorizing bodies, such as an Annual Conference.

Council, Administrative.

See *Administrative Council.*

Council of Bishops.

All active and retired bishops of The United Methodist Church. The Council of Bishops meets twice a year. It plans for "the general oversight and promotion of the temporal and spiritual interests of the entire Church and for carrying into effect the rules, regulations, and responsibilities prescribed and enjoined by the General Conference" (*Book of Discipline*). Retired bishops have the right of voice but not vote in the deliberations of the Council.

Council on Finance and Administration, Annual Conference.

See *Finance and Administration, Annual Conference Council on.*

Council on Finance and Administration, General.

See *Finance and Administration, General Council on.*

Council on Ministries, Annual Conference.

See *Ministries, Annual Conference Council on.*

Council on Ministries, General.

See *Ministries, General Council on.*

Council on Ministries, local church.

See *Ministries, local church Council on.*

course of study. The educational requirements that must be completed by a person seeking to be a local pastor or to enter the ordained ministry, but who has not attended theological school. A course of study is required to qualify for a license to preach. This is followed by a five-year course of study. These courses are developed under the direction of the Division of Ordained Ministry of the General Board of Higher Education and Ministry. The courses of study are no longer the primary path for persons entering the ordained ministry. They continue to provide an entry, however, into Annual Conference membership for persons who have not met the regular educational requirements of theological education but whose ministry has warranted special consideration.

71

covenant. The entering into and committing oneself to a continuing relationship. Christians see themselves as a people of a covenant with God. The New Testament or "New Covenant" is that covenant of the saving work of Jesus Christ through the grace of God and the response Christians make in their profession of faith and baptism. This understanding of covenant has been important through the life of United Methodism.

Covenant Discipleship.
The program adapting the early Methodist class meetings of John Wesley to the life and work of today's congregation. Covenant Discipleship groups use the objective and dynamic of the class meeting, mutual support, and disciplined method to offer a weekly point of accountability for those who are called to a committed Christian discipleship. Each group uses a written covenant of intent, which the members write, incorporating the General Rules of the early Methodist societies. A group consists of up to seven members and meets once a week for one hour.

Covenant Service, Wesley's.
The renewal of the individual's covenant with God through a service that was established and emphasized by John Wesley. He believed that Methodists, and all Christians, should reaffirm their covenant with God annually. In 1755 John Wesley held his first covenant service using words written earlier by Richard Alleine. Wesley published this service in a pamphlet in 1780, and this form was used without alteration for nearly a century in England. It has been modified somewhat in more recent years. The covenant hymn, "Come, Let Us Use the Grace Divine," was written for this service by Charles Wesley. The service is included in *The Book of Worship* under the title

"An Order of Worship for Such as Would Enter into or Renew Their Covenant with God—For Use in a Watch Night Service, on the first Sunday of the Year, or Other Occasion." This Covenant Service is often used in United Methodism as a Watch Night service on New Year's Eve. The Covenant Service is observed in some local churches on New Year's Day or on the first Sunday in January. The service focuses on the Christian's renewing the covenant of response to the grace of God in Christ.

crèche. ('kresh) A nativity scene representing the stable in Bethlehem with the Christ child, Mary, and Joseph. Many crèches also have figures of the shepherds, the wise men, and various animals.

credentials. The official certificates or documents in The United Methodist Church attesting to receiving a license to preach, to consecration as a bishop or a diaconal minister, or to ordination as a minister. In the case of a bishop, the election and consecration certificate is signed by members of the Council of Bishops. *The Book of Discipline* contains many provisions for how these credentials are to be given and recognized and under what conditions they are to be surrendered.

creed. A brief, authoritative statement of religious belief. Historically, the two most important of these for United Methodism have been the Apostles' Creed and the Nicene Creed.

cremation. The burning of the body of a deceased person. Although cremation is not usually performed on deceased United Methodists, it is considered an acceptable practice.

crosier. ('krō -zhər) One of the traditional symbols of the office of bishop. A crosier is a long staff that may have a curve or crook at the end, symbolizing the shepherd's crook, which was used to guide and assist the sheep. As such it became the symbol for the pastoral office and more particularly for the bishop as the shepherd of the believers. Although the crosier has long been in use in the liturgical churches such as the Roman Catholic Church, the Orthodox churches, and the Anglican churches, it has only recently come into usage in The United Methodist Church. It is more common now than formerly that a new United Methodist bishop is given a crosier at the time of consecration.

cross. The central symbol of Christianity. The cross is the symbol of Christ's death and resurrection and of the

gospel of redemption made possible by Christ. Most United Methodist churches have a cross on the Lord's table (communion table) or mounted on the front wall of the sanctuary.

crucifer. The person who carries a cross at the head of a procession in worship services.

Cup, the. The name given to the chalice which holds the wine for the Sacrament of Holy Communion. It is placed on the Lord's table (communion table) and is used by the minister in the Sacrament. The word also refers to the individual cups used by each worshiper.
    See also *chalice.*

curriculum resources. The printed and other resources designed and made available to help local United Methodist churches carry out the educational ministry with children, youth, young adults, adults, and families. Curriculum resources are also developed to meet the needs of the various racial, ethnic, age, cultural, and language constituencies of The United Methodist Church. Curriculum resources are designed for use in a variety of settings, both formal and informal, including Sunday schools, fellowship groups, outdoor experiences, family life, and confirmation classes. Curriculum resources are developed under the direction of the Curriculum Resources Committee, which is related to both the General Board of Discipleship and The United Methodist Publishing House.

Daily Christian Advocate, The.
See *Advocate, The Christian*.

deacon. An ordained minister who has progressed sufficiently in preparation for ministry to be received by an Annual Conference as either a probationary member or an associate member. A deacon has the authority to conduct divine worship, to preach the Word, to perform the marriage ceremony where the laws of the state permit, and to bury the dead. When invited to do so by an elder, the deacon may assist in the administration of the Sacraments. A deacon is ordained by a bishop using the Order of Service for the Ordination of Deacons.

deaconess. A woman who in response to God's call devotes her life to service in the church. Deaconesses are approved by the General Board of Global Ministries and commissioned by a bishop. They may serve in any capacity not requiring full clergy rights. Full-time service is the norm for a deaconess. The appointment to a place of service is made by a bishop.

dedication of church property. The devoting
of United Methodist Church properties exclusively to
God's service. Dedication, from the Latin *dedicatio*, is
the act of setting apart for a specific use. Before any
church building, parsonage, or other church unit is formally dedicated, all financial obligations and debts
must be paid. *The Book of Worship* (1969) contains offices
or services for the conducting of the dedication of a
church building. There are also services for the dedication of a school or college building, a hospital, a church
organ, and memorials.

deed, church property.
See *trust clause in deeds.*

deeds of trust.
See *trust clause in deeds.*

delegates, Annual Conference.
See *membership, Annual Conference.*

delegates, General Conference. The voting
members of the General Conference. The total number
of delegates to a General Conference must consist of an
equal number of clergy and lay delegates. Lay delegates
are elected by ballot by the lay members of their respective Annual Conferences. Clergy delegates are elected
by ballot by the clergy members. These elections are
held during the sessions of the Annual Conference in
the year preceding the General Conference. The number
of delegates an Annual Conference is entitled to send to
a General Conference is based on two factors: the number of clergy members of the Annual Conference and the
number of members of local churches in the Annual
Conference. The Constitution of The United Methodist

Church states that the membership of General Conference shall be no fewer than 600 and no more than 1,000. Since 1968 the practice has been to have the total number of delegates at or near the upper limit.

delegates, Jurisdictional Conference. The voting members of a Jurisdictional Conference. The total membership of a Jurisdictional Conference must consist of an equal number of clergy and lay delegates. Lay delegates are elected by ballot by the lay members of their respective Annual Conferences. Clergy delegates are elected by ballot by the clergy members. These elections are held during the sessions of the Annual Conference in the year preceding the Jurisdictional Conference. The number of delegates an Annual Conference is entitled to send to a Jurisdictional Conference is determined by two factors: the number of clergy members of the Annual Conference and the number of members of the local churches of the Annual Conference. The total number of delegates sent to each of the five Jurisdictional Conferences varies because of the differences in total number of lay and clergy members in the Annual Conferences of the jurisdictions. Those persons elected by the Annual Conferences as delegates to a General Conference are also considered to be first elected delegates of their respective Annual Conferences to the Jurisdictional Conference.

denomination. The body of persons or the organization formed around a particular set of religious beliefs or structure or type of government. In the United States, various religious bodies, such as The United Methodist Church, are referred to as denominations. Sometimes they are also referred to as communions.

diaconal minister. A person whose life is committed to professional and full-time ministry in The United Methodist Church in response to God's call. *Diaconal* derives from the Greek word *diakonia*, which means service.

Diaconal ministers are called to specialized ministries of service, justice, and love within local congregations and the broader world. They have met the standards set by the General Conference, the Division of Diaconal Ministry, and the Annual Conference Board of Diaconal Ministry. They are consecrated by a bishop at a session of the Annual Conference.

Diaconal Ministry, Annual Conference Board of. The agency in the Annual Conference charged with responsibility for the candidacy, Annual Conference relationships, and other matters pertaining to diaconal ministers. The Annual Conference Board of Diaconal Ministry recommends to the Annual Conference those persons who are to be elected to serve as diaconal ministers.

director. In the local church, a lay person or specialized minister who is certified as having the proper qualifications to lead the program in Christian education, music, evangelism, and so forth.

In the Annual Conference, the title generally refers to the Director of the Council on Ministries. The director is the person who is in charge of the work and staff of the Council.

In a general agency, the director is a person in charge of a department or a major work portfolio.

disability, ministerial. The status granted to ministerial members of an Annual Conference when they are forced to give up their work because of physical or emotional disability. They may be granted this leave without changing their membership relationship in the Annual Conference.

The leave can be granted only upon review and approval of the Conference Board of Ordained Ministry, the Conference Board of Pensions, and a majority vote of the clergy members of the Annual Conference. Similar provisions exist for disability leaves for bishops, diaconal ministers, local pastors, and lay employees. These are governed by their respective authorizing bodies and regulations.

discipleship. The active living of the individual Christian in accordance with the teachings of Jesus Christ, that is, being as effective a disciple of Christ as possible. Discipleship involves a ministry of outreaching love and witness to others concerning Christ and God's grace. Discipleship also calls the Christian to ministries of servanthood and service in the world to the glory of God and for human fulfillment.

Discipleship, General Board of. The agency established by the General Conference whose chief purpose is to assist Annual Conferences, districts, and local churches in their efforts to win persons to Jesus Christ as his disciples. It provides leadership and resources in the following areas: spiritual growth and development, devotional literature, curriculum resources, Christian education, evangelism, worship, stewardship, ministry of the laity, United Methodist Men. The Board places a strong emphasis on strengthening the Christian life and mission of the local church and its members. Its offices are in Nashville, Tennessee.

The Book of Discipline also provides that there shall be

a Board of Discipleship in each Annual Conference to address these same purposes and subject areas.

Discipleship Resources. The publishing unit of the General Board of Discipleship which publishes and distributes resources to assist Annual Conferences, local churches, and individual United Methodists to carry forward programs of outreach and service. Its offices are in Nashville, Tennessee.

disciplinary. In United Methodist usage, the reference to a statement or provision being in accordance with the Constitution and the laws of The United Methodist Church as contained in *The Book of Discipline.*

discipline. A term with three distinct meanings in United Methodism. First, early Methodists acquired a reputation for having strict patterns and rules for regulating their daily and spiritual lives. This "discipline" became characteristic of the movement in its early years in England and the United States. This is outlined in the General Rules.

Second, the word relates to the constancy of practice and organizational form that has been maintained through the years. The denomination often describes itself as one under the guidance and discipline of its sense of personal requirements and organizational rules.

Third, *The Discipline* is the shortened, commonly used name for the book containing the law, doctrine, administrative, and organizational guidelines for the denomination.

Discipline, The Book of. The fundamental book outlining the law, doctrine, administration, and organizational work and procedures for The United Methodist Church. The book was officially called *The Doctrines and Discipline* until 1968, when it was given its present name. It contains the Constitution, the Articles of Religion and Confession of Faith, the General Rules, and provisions for the organization and administration of local churches, Annual Conferences, and general agencies, as well as outlining the regulations for ordained, diaconal, and other ministers.

Each General Conference amends *The Book of Discipline,* and the actions of the General Conference are reflected in the quadrennial revision.

discontinue a local church.

The closing of a local church that is no longer viable. Often this occurs when the membership and participation have diminished to the point that effective ministry is no longer taking place. Those members remaining on the roll of a church to be discontinued are to be transferred to another United Methodist church (usually one close by) or to other churches as the members themselves may select. The action to discontinue a local church is made by vote of an Annual Conference upon the recommendation of the district superintendent. When a church is discontinued, a pastor is no longer appointed, services are stopped, and the property may be sold.

district.

A definite geographical and administrative subdivision of an Annual Conference. The number of districts is determined by the Annual Conference. The boundaries of the districts are determined by the bishop after consultation with the district superintendents. A district consists of all the pastoral charges within its boundaries and is under the supervision of a district superintendent.

District Conference. The meeting held to conduct necessary work of the district. The Annual Conference determines what the membership of a District Conference shall be. Generally, it consists of the clergy of the district and one or more delegates from each pastoral charge. It is presided over by the district superintendent.

district superintendent. An ordained minister appointed by a bishop to oversee the pastors and local churches in a district. A district superintendent may not serve in that capacity more than six years in any consecutive nine years. No minister may serve more than a total of twelve years as a superintendent. The superintendent carries a wide range of responsibilities for the local churches in the district and throughout the Conference as a whole. Primary responsibilities relate to overseeing the work of the local churches, including presiding at Charge Conferences, and supervising the work of the pastors, including participating with the bishop in the making of appointments.

doctrinal standards, the. Key statements of historical and doctrinal importance for The United Methodist Church. The doctrinal standards include the Articles of Religion and the Confession of Faith. These are accompanied by the General Rules of Our United Societies. All three of these are printed in *The Book of Discipline* and are protected by the Restrictive Rules. Part 2 of *The Book of Discipline,* in sections entitled "Our Doctrinal Heritage" and "Our Doctrinal History," provides a statement that serves as an excellent background for an understanding of the doctrinal standards.

See also *Articles of Religion; Confession of Faith, the;* and *General Rules, the.*

dossal. A drapery hanging behind and above the Lord's table (communion table).

doxology. In general usage, a short statement of praise, glory, and thanksgiving to God. It is often a short hymn designed to be sung by the worshiping congregation.

The doxology most familiar to United Methodists is the hymn "Old 100th" with the opening line, "Praise God, from whom all blessings flow." In many United Methodist churches, this is listed in worship bulletins as "The Doxology" and is sung by the congregation as the offering is brought forward.

E

Easter. The day in the Christian calendar that celebrates the resurrection of Jesus Christ. Easter is the most important day in the calendar. It is celebrated on the first Sunday after the full moon on or after March 21; therefore, the date varies from March 22 to April 25.

See also *calendar, Christian.*

Easter Season. The season of fifty days from Easter to Pentecost Day. Easter Season is very important in the Christian calendar because it celebrates on the one hand the risen Christ with his appearances and teachings and on the other hand the beginnings of the Christian church. Historically, the term *Pentecost* was used to refer not only to the last day in the fifty days between Easter and Pentecost, but also to the entire period as well. Now the practice is to reserve the term for Pentecost Sunday and to refer to the fifty-day period as the Easter Season.

Easter Vigil. A service beginning on Saturday night and lasting until early Easter morning. The service may also be held before dawn on Easter Sunday morning. The principal portions of the Easter Vigil are:

1. The Service of Light
2. The Service of the Word
3. The Service of the Water
4. The Service of the Bread and Cup.

The Easter Vigil is a service with a long history in the Christian church.

ecumenical. From the Greek word meaning the whole inhabited earth. Ecumenical thought and action pertains to the given oneness and wholeness of the Christian church, the body of Christ. It involves dialogue and joint action among various sectors of the Christian community; the healing of divisions and the elimination of divisiveness among Christian churches; efforts toward unification of membership and ministries for worship and witness in a more truly inclusive fellowship. The United Methodist Church has been active in many efforts and organizations related to ecumenical issues and endeavors.

education, local church work area on. The work area on education established to design and recommend to the local church Council on Ministries the organization and content of the educational program. It is to ensure that persons of all ages are provided with opportunities to study the Bible and the Christian faith and life and to facilitate the use of United Methodist curricula and resources.

educational leave.
See *study leave.*

eight-year rule. The General Conference rule stating that a voting member of a general agency may serve no more than two consecutive four-year terms on that agency. Although they are not required to do so, most Annual Conferences have adopted the eight-year rule for membership on Conference agencies.

elder. The name given to the higher order of the ordained ministry in The United Methodist Church. Elders are clergy who have completed their formal preparation for the ministry of Word, Sacrament, and Order; have been elected itinerant ministers in full connection in an Annual Conference; and have been ordained elders. In American Methodism it has always been the practice to confer the Order of Elder first by the vote of the clergy members of the Annual Conference and then by the formal rite of ordination with the laying on of hands by a bishop and other elders. Elders at ordination are given a certificate of ordination, the credentials, and are authorized to exercise the power and privileges of ordination for life through the whole of the denomination.

See also *credentials; full connection, minister in;* and *laying on of hands.*

elements. The term used to refer to the bread and wine used in the Sacrament of the Lord's Supper.

Epiphany. January 6, which marks the end of the Christmas Season or Christmastide. In the Western churches, Epiphany Day has marked the observance of the arrival of the wise men. In the earliest Christian traditions, maintained by the Eastern churches, the day began a period that celebrated the incarnation and baptism of Christ. The liturgical color for Epiphany Day is white.

87

Epiphany, Season After. The season from January 7 through the day before Ash Wednesday. It may include anywhere from four to nine Sundays, depending on the date of Easter. The liturgical colors for the Season after Epiphany are white for the first Sunday (Baptism of the Lord) and last Sunday (Transfiguration) and green for the rest of the season.

episcopacy. Refers to the office of bishop. Episcopacy also refers to the system of church government in which bishops serve as general superintendents of the church and are responsible individually and collectively for the spiritual and temporal welfare of the denomination. The episcopal system is established by the Constitution as an integral part of the organizational structure of United Methodism.

Episcopal Address, The. An important address given in one of the early sessions of each General Conference by one of the active bishops on behalf of the Council of Bishops. This has been done since 1812. The address reviews the state of the denomination and speaks to the future needs and directions for United Methodism. One bishop is selected by the Council of Bishops to present the address and to prepare an initial draft. This is critiqued by the members of the Council and perfected. Upon approval by the Council, it is then presented to the General Conference.

episcopal area.
See *area, episcopal*.

Episcopal Fund. The general fund that provides for the salary and expenses of the active bishops and for the support of retired bishops and their spouses.

episcopal residence. The residence provided for each active bishop within the episcopal area to which he or she is assigned. The Annual Conference or Conferences of the episcopal area are responsible for the purchase of a residence. The annual cost for the maintenance and upkeep of the residence is paid in part by the Annual Conference or Conferences involved and the Episcopal Fund.

Epworth. A small town in northeast Lincolnshire, England, that was the birthplace of John and Charles Wesley. Their father, Samuel Wesley, was the Church of England rector of the Epworth parish. The Wesley home, the Epworth rectory, still stands and is a focal point for Methodists when visiting there. The Epworth League was the name of the youth organization from 1890 until the Methodist Youth Fellowship was created. Epworth is still commonly used as the name for a local United Methodist church.

Equalization Rule, Annual Conference.
Requires that the number of lay voting members of an Annual Conference equal the number of ministerial voting members. This provision is found in Article 35 of the Constitution of The United Methodist Church. The clergy membership includes all ministers in full connection, active and retired, probationary members, associate members, affiliate members, and local pastors under full-time appointment. The lay membership consists of a lay member elected by each pastoral charge, diaconal ministers, Conference and district lay leaders, and persons holding specific offices in the Annual Conference. If the above group of lay members does not equal the number of clergy members, the Annual Con-

ference by its own formula will provide for the election of additional lay members to remove the imbalance.

equitable salaries. The procedure for establishing minimum salary schedules in an Annual Conference for pastors. The Annual Conference Commission on Equitable Salaries is responsible for recommending the salary schedules and standards to the Annual Conference.

Local churches not able to pay the full amount of the equitable or minimum salary may receive salary supplement funds from the Annual Conference. These funds are provided through the Equitable Salary Fund, which is apportioned to all of the local churches.

Eucharist.
See *Lord's Supper, Sacrament of the.*

evaluation. The procedure recommended in *The Book of Discipline* for many areas of the life of the denomination in which a person, program, or agency is evaluated against measurable goals. The evaluation may be performed either by peers, a committee established for the purpose, or outside consultants. The local congregation is to be evaluated by the Administrative Board. The general program-related agencies are evaluated by the General Council on Ministries.

Performance evaluation for ministry is undertaken by the Committee on Pastor-Parish Relations in the local church and by the Cabinet. District superintendents are evaluated by the district Committee on the District Superintendency. Bishops are evaluated by the area Committee on Episcopacy.

Evangelical Association, The; The Evangelical Church. Founded in the early 1800s by

Jacob Albright to serve the German population in Pennsylvania. Albright was influenced by the preaching of Philip Otterbein and by his experiences in a Methodist class meeting. About 1796 Albright began to travel and preach throughout central Pennsylvania. In 1803 he was ordained at a small conference, which took the name The Albright's People. In 1807 at the first regular conference of the group, the name was changed to The Newly-Formed Methodist Church. The first General Conference was held in 1816 at which the name was changed to The Evangelical Association, a hymnal adopted, and a *Discipline* developed. The church spread westward primarily serving the German-speaking population. In 1894 a serious rift split the church and it was not until 1922 that the two groups were reunited, taking the name The Evangelical Church. In 1933 the denomination began serious merger discussions with The Church of the United Brethren in Christ. These two united in 1946 to form The Evangelical United Brethren Church.

Evangelical United Brethren Church, The.

Formed in 1946 by the union of The Church of the United Brethren in Christ and The Evangelical Church. Both denominations began as churches serving the German population in the early 1800s. By the time of the 1946 union, these churches had broadened their ministries throughout the eastern and the north central portions of the United States. The general church offices for the EUB church were located in Dayton, Ohio. Discussions soon began concerning union with The Methodist Church. A plan of union was approved by both denominations. In 1968 The Evangelical United Brethren Church and The Methodist Church united to form The United Methodist Church.

evangelism. The winning of persons to Jesus Christ as Savior and Lord. From the Latin word *evangelium*, meaning good news or gospel, evangelism is the proclamation of the gospel to individuals and groups by preaching, teaching, and personal or family visitation. It is the seeking by the Christian to bring others into a vital personal relationship with Christ.

evangelist. In the broad sense, any individual who actively seeks to bring another into a vital relationship with Christ. Often this is through the conversion of the person to the Christian faith. In a narrower sense, evangelist has been applied to ministers who actively preach personal conversion.

Within the policies of The United Methodist Church, the term *evangelist* or *Conference-approved evangelist* has a specific meaning. A Conference-approved evangelist is a person who has met the standards set for approved evangelists by the General Board of Discipleship, the Conference Board of Discipleship, and the Conference Board of Ordained Ministry. These evangelists are authorized to conduct services in the churches of the Annual Conference as requested.

executive session, Annual Conference. The meeting of only the ministerial members of an Annual Conference. Associate members and preparatory members may attend, but they may not vote on certain items coming before the executive session. The ministers in executive session vote on matters relating to ordination, ministerial membership and relationships in the Annual Conference, and the character of the clergy.

Finance and Administration, Annual Conference Council on.
The primary fiscal agency for the Annual Conference. The Annual Conference Council on Finance and Administration is responsible for the development and oversight of the fiscal and administrative policies of the Annual Conference. The Council recommends the budgets of income and expenditures for the Conference and oversees the receipt and disbursement of Conference funds.

Finance and Administration, General Council on.
Established by the General Conference to coordinate and administer the finances of the denomination as approved by the General Conference. The General Council on Finance and Administration serves as the central treasurer of the denomination. As such it receives and disburses all general funds. The general agencies are accountable to the Council for their fiscal administration. The Council reports to and receives direction from the General Conference.

fiscal year.
Determined by the General Conference for The United Methodist Church to be the same as the calendar year, January 1 through December 31.

font, baptismal. A special container used to hold the water for the Sacrament of Baptism. The font is often mounted on a pedestal. Generally, in United Methodist churches the baptismal font is found in the front of the church, often inside the chancel railing.

Forum for Scriptural Christianity. The formal name of the unofficial organization of United Methodists that focuses on evangelical and renewal issues within The United Methodist Church. It is more commonly known as Good News, which is also the name of its bimonthly magazine. The Forum for Scriptural Christianity also publishes books and resources for local churches including curriculum. Its offices are in Wilmore, Kentucky.

See also *Good News.*

founding date, Annual Conference or local church. The date on which an Annual Conference or local church was first organized. If two or more Annual Conferences or local churches with different founding dates unite or merge, the founding date for the new Conference or local church is to be the date of the older or oldest of the uniting groups.

founding date, the denomination's. The date of the organization of the first of the antecedent denominations of The United Methodist Church. The Methodist Episcopal Church was organized in 1784 at the Christmas Conference in Baltimore, Maryland. Therefore, 1784 is accepted as the founding date for The United Methodist Church.

full connection, minister in. A historic phrase within United Methodism denoting the person who is a ministerial member of an Annual Conference. As such the clergy member has been voted by the ministerial members of the Conference to be a full member and is thereby eligible for ordination as an elder. Members in full connection have the right to vote on all matters in the Annual Conference except the election of lay delegates to General or Jurisdictional Conferences.

full member, local church.
See *membership, local church.*

Full Membership Roll.
See *membership roll.*

funds, general.
See *general funds.*

95

General Administration Fund. Provides for the expenses of administrative functions at the general level of the church. These include the expenses for the General Conference, the Judicial Council, special commissions and committees established by the General Conference, and other administrative activities as are recommended for inclusion by the General Council on Finance and Administration and approved by the General Conference.

general agencies.
See *agencies, general.*

General Conference. The highest legislative body in the denomination. The Constitution states: "The General Conference shall have full legislative power over all matters distinctively connectional." It meets in April or May once every four years for a two-week period. A General Conference may vote to have an adjourned session, if it is deemed necessary. Bishops preside at the sessions of the General Conference but do not have the privilege of voice or vote in its deliberations. The General Conference is composed of an equal number of lay and clergy delegates elected by their respective Annual Conferences. The clergy and lay delegates debate and vote as one body. The primary responsibility of the General Conference is to enact legislation that establishes the conditions for membership, defines the powers and duties of the clergy, defines the powers and duties of the Conferences, establishes the powers and duties of the bishops, provides for a judicial system within the church, establishes the budget for the denomination, and establishes legislation governing the work of the local church and the general agencies.

general funds. Those funds approved by the General Conference for the support of various aspects of the work of the denomination. These funds are either apportioned to the Annual Conferences (and thence to the local churches) or are raised through special offerings. The General Council on Finance and Administration serves as the treasurer of general church funds. As such it receives the funds from the local churches and Annual Conferences and disburses them under the provisions established by the General Conference.

general ministry. The phrase which for United Methodists means that "all Christians are called to minister wherever Christ would have them serve and witness in deeds and words that heal and free" *(The Book of Discipline)*. This general ministry of all Christians is a gift of the grace of God and is a task to which Christians are called to respond.

General Minutes, the. Compiled and published annually by the Council on Finance and Administration under the full title, *The General Minutes of the Annual Conferences of The United Methodist Church*. The volume contains statistical information for every pastoral charge in the Annual Conferences in the United States and Puerto Rico. It also contains summary statistics for the Annual Conferences in the Central Conferences. *The General Minutes* also contains for each Annual Conference in the United States the place, date, and name of the presiding bishop for the Conference session, the information on the ministerial relationships to the Conference, and the appointment list of ministers to their pastoral charges. Also included are an index of all ministers and specialized lists of diaconal ministers, deaconesses, and home missionaries, and chaplains. The decisions of the Judicial Council for the year are also printed in full.

General Rules, the.

A set of rules devised in 1738 by John Wesley for his societies. He did this to make clear the connection between the saving faith and Christian behavior and to indicate what was expected of persons as they became members of the Methodist Societies. In 1743 he published these in a pamphlet entitled *The Nature, Design, and General Rules of the United Societies*. The General Rules were approved by the American Methodist church in 1785. Thomas Coke and Francis Asbury prepared a revised edition, which has continued to be published as a part of *The Book of Discipline*. These rules are no longer enforced. The regulation that these should be read to each congregation once a quarter has been discontinued. The General Rules, however, are protected by Restrictive Rule of the Constitution. As a consequence, they may not be revoked or changed.

See also *Restrictive Rules, the*.

general secretary. The highest ranking staff officer and chief administrative staff person of a general agency. An exception is the General Board of Publication, in which the office is called President and Publisher.

General Services, the. Those services of worship which have been approved and made a part of the Ritual of The United Methodist Church by the 1984 General Conference. The General Services contain the directions and text for conducting the basic services of the Ritual for the denomination. These are included in *The United Methodist Hymnal* (1989 ed.). The General Services include the following: The Basic Pattern of Worship, An Order of Sunday Worship, Services of Word and Table (the Sacrament of the Lord's Supper), Services of the Baptismal Covenant, A Service of Christian Marriage, and A Service of Death and Resurrection.

Global Ministries, General Board of. The agency, established by the General Conference, whose chief purpose is to be the missional instrument of The United Methodist Church throughout the world. It has a prime responsibility to witness to Jesus Christ throughout the world, to recruit and send missionaries, to raise the awareness and support of persons in local churches for the requirements of global mission, and to assist in the development of Christian churches and leadership. It organizes its work through three principal program divisions, National, Women's, and World, and four principal departments, Health and Welfare Ministries, Mission Education and Cultivation, Mission Personnel Resources, and the United Methodist Committee on Relief. Its offices are in New York City.

The Book of Discipline also provides that in each Annual Conference there shall be a Board of Global Ministries and a United Methodist Women's organization to address these same purposes and issues.

gloria in excelsis Deo. ('glōr-ē-ə-,in-eks-'chel-səs-,dā-[,]-ō)(Glory be to God on high) The opening Latin words of the traditional hymn often sung as a part of the Sacrament of the Lord's Supper. The words for the text: "Glory be to God on high, and on earth peace, good will to all" come from Luke 2:14 and John 1:29.

gloria Patri. ('glōr-ē-ə-'pä-[,]trē)(Glory be to the Father) The opening Latin words for the widely used short hymn of praise to the Trinity. The familiar words are "Glory be to the Father, and to the Son, and to the Holy Ghost; as it was in the beginning, is now, and ever shall be, world without end." The words are those of a doxology which has been in use in the church from the third or fourth century. The *Gloria Patri* is often sung by the congregation immediately following an affirmation of faith or a reading of Scripture.

Golden Cross Sunday. Observed in The United Methodist Church each year on the first Sunday in May. The observance of the Sunday focuses upon the work of health and welfare ministries and institutions in the Annual Conference. If the Annual Conference so directs, an offering may be received in the local churches of the Conference for the support of the health and welfare ministries.

Good Friday. The Friday before Easter on which the crucifixion of Jesus is remembered. Good Friday

services focus upon prayerful reflection on the death of Christ and penance and special devotion for the believer.

Good News. The commonly used name for the Forum for Scriptural Christianity and its constituents, as well as the Forum's bimonthly magazine, *Good News*. See also *Forum for Scriptural Christianity; gospel*.

gospel. From the Latin *evangelium*, meaning good tale or good news. Gospel has a number of distinct meanings. It refers to the Good News concerning Christ, the Kingdom of God, and salvation. It also refers to the teachings of Jesus and the apostles. The word is used in connection with the first four books of the New Testament. For example, the Gospel of Mark or the Gospel according to Mark refers to the New Testament book ascribed to Mark in which the life and teachings of Jesus are described. In services of worship, the Reading from the Gospel or the Gospel Reading refers to the Scripture reading from one of the four Gospels.

grace, table. A prayer, immediately prior to a meal, asking the blessing of God for the food and of thanksgiving.

Graded Press. Within The United Methodist Publishing House, the name used for the unit that has had responsibility for the printing, sales, and distribution of the church school curriculum of The United Methodist Church, available through Cokesbury.

Great Thanksgiving, the. The name now given to that portion of the Service of Word and Table (the Sacrament of the Lord's Supper) which contains the words of consecration. *The United Methodist Hymnal* uses the Great Thanksgiving as the heading for that portion of the Service of Word and Table (the Sacrament of the Lord's Supper) which begins with the Sursum Corda, includes the words of consecration, and ends with the Lord's Prayer.

H

handicapping conditions, persons with.
Persons with a disability or difference in appearance or behavior that restricts mobility, communication, intellectual comprehension, or personal relationships, and interferes with the person's participation or that of his or her family in the life of the church. Persons with handicapping conditions are not to be discriminated against by any local church, agency, or institution of The United Methodist Church.

hands, laying on of.
See *laying on of hands.*

Heritage Sunday.
The Sunday designated by the General Conference as a day for the church to remember the past by committing itself to the continuing call of God. Heritage Sunday is to be observed on April 23 (the date in 1968 of the church union that created The United Methodist Church) or the Sunday following that date. The observance is under the general supervision of the General Commission on Archives and History.

Higher Education and Campus Ministry, local church work area on. The work area that is to keep the local church Council on Ministries or Administrative Council and the entire congregation informed of higher education concerns. It is to devise plans to minister to college students and faculty related to the local church. It is to interpret the programs of the denomination regarding its colleges, universities, scholarship and grant programs.

Higher Education and Ministry, General Board of. The agency, established by the General Conference, whose chief purpose is to prepare and assist persons to fulfill their ordained and diaconal ministries and to provide general oversight and care for campus ministries and institutions of higher education, including schools, colleges, universities, and theological schools. It carries out its work through four principal divisions, Chaplains and Related Ministries, Higher Education, Diaconal Ministry, and Ordained Ministry. Its offices are in Nashville, Tennessee.

The *Book of Discipline* also provides that there shall be a Board of Diaconal Ministry, a Board of Ordained Ministry, and a Board of Higher Education and Campus Ministry in each Annual Conference.

historic landmarks.
See *landmarks.*

historic shrines.
See *shrine.*

historic sites.
See *site.*

Holy Communion.
See *Lord's Supper, Sacrament of the.*

Holy Thursday.
The Thursday of Holy Week, the day on which the Last Supper and the institution of the Lord's Supper is commemorated. Since the Gospel of John records that the Last Supper included Jesus' washing of the disciples' feet, in some churches the ceremony of footwashing also is observed on this day. Holy Thursday is also referred to as Maundy Thursday.

Holy Week.
The week of Christian observances leading to Easter Sunday. It begins with Palm Sunday and progresses through Holy or Maundy Thursday and Good Friday. It culminates with the Easter Sunday celebrations.

home missionary.
The title given to a person who, in response to God's call and on recommendation of the Mission Personnel Resources Department of the General Board of Global Ministries, has been commissioned by a bishop. These persons are assigned to ministries within the United States. Either a lay or a clergy person may be a home missionary.

honorable location of clergy.
See *location of clergy, honorable.*

hosanna.
An acclamation of praise and adoration to God. It comes from the Greek word *hosanna*, which serves as a translation for the Hebrew phrase meaning "save now, we pray." Its usage in the church is as an expression of enthusiastic praise, especially on Palm Sunday, as in Mark 11:9, "Hosanna! Blessed is he who comes in the name of the Lord!"

Human Relations Day. A special Sunday autho-rized by the General Conference to be observed with an offering taken throughout the denomination dur-ing the season of Epiphany on the Sunday before the observance of Martin Luther King, Jr.'s, birthday. Human Relations Day calls upon United Methodists to further the development of improved race rela-tions. One aspect of this is the funding, through the offering, of programs determined by the General Conference. The funds are administered by the gener-al agencies under which the approved programs are lodged.

Humble Access, Prayer of. A traditional prayer said by the congregation as a part of the ritual for the Lord's Supper. It begins with the words, "We do not presume to come to this thy table, O merciful Lord." *The United Methodist Hymnal* (1989) contains four numbered services for communion. These are each called "A Service of Word and Table" (replacing "The Order for the Administration of the Sacrament of the Lord's Supper or Holy Communion"). The Prayer of Humble Access is retained in "A Service of Word and Table IV," which retains the traditional text from the rituals of the former Methodist and former Evangeli-cal United Brethren churches.

hymn, hymnal. The first, a religious poem set to music so that it may be sung during worship. The sec-ond, a collection of hymns printed and bound together for use in congregational and private worship. The singing of hymns has been an important part of the Methodist tradition. Charles Wesley wrote a great many hymns that reflected the theology of the Wes-leyan movement.

106

Hymnal, The United Methodist. The name of the new hymnal of The United Methodist Church. More than four years in preparation, the new hymnal was approved by the 1988 General Conference and was published in 1989.

Hymnals have been important in the life of the Wesleyan movement. John Wesley published his first hymnal in 1737 in South Carolina. The various predecessor denominations of The United Methodist Church all regularly published and revised hymnals for their worship use. The 1960 General Conference of The Methodist Church authorized a revision of its hymnal, which was completed in 1966. At the time of the 1968 union, the hymnal of The Evangelical United Brethren Church and the 1966 hymnal of The Methodist Church were recognized as official hymnals of the new denomination. *The United Methodist Hymnal* is the first official hymnal to be authorized by and prepared for The United Methodist Church.

I

inclusiveness. The term in United Methodism that means that every level of the denomination is to be open to all people in all settings on a fully equal basis. There is to be no distinction made because of racial or ethnic background, national origin, gender, age, handicapping condition, or any other criteria. It is the policy of The United Methodist Church to be fully inclusive of all persons in their participation in the life and work of the church.

intercession. Prayers or petitions on behalf of a person, a group of persons, or general needs of the world. Prayers of intercession are an integral part of personal and congregational worship.

Interdenominational Cooperation Fund. One of the general funds of The United Methodist Church authorized by the General Conference. The purpose of the fund is to provide the United Methodist share of the budgets of organizations that relate to the ecumenical responsibilities of the denomination. Recommendations regarding the amount to be raised are made by the Council of Bishops and the General Commission on Christian Unity and Interreligious Concerns. Monies from this fund go to the National Council of the Churches of Christ, the World Council of Churches, and the Consultation on Church Union.

Interpreter, The. The official program journal of The United Methodist Church, published by United Methodist Communications. *The Interpreter* informs pastors and lay leadership about the church program and promotes the general funds of the denomination.

intinction. A method of partaking of the elements in the Sacrament of the Lord's Supper. In this procedure, the participant takes the bread and dips it into the wine in a large chalice held by the pastor. The participant then eats the moistened bread.

invitation to Christian discipleship. The invitation given by a pastor to those who would make a decision to declare their faith in Christ or join the church or both. The invitation is generally given following the sermon and before the singing of the closing hymn. Those who would make a decision are asked to come forward to the chancel railing. The invitation reflects the historic United Methodist tradition of an "altar call."

invocation. In United Methodist usage, a prayer asking for a special sense of God's presence and guidance. The invocation is offered at an early point in a service of worship or at the beginning of a meeting or other event.

involuntary retirement.
  See *retirement, involuntary.*

itineracy, itinerancy. The system in The United Methodist Church by which ministers are appointed to their charges by the bishops. The ministers are under obligation to serve where appointed. The present form of the itineracy grew from the practice of Methodist pastors traveling widely throughout the church on circuits. Assigned to service by a bishop, they were not to remain with one particular congregation for any length of time.

J

Journal, Annual Conference.
See *Conference Journal.*

Journal, General Conference.
See *Conference Journal.*

Judicial Council. The highest judicial body or "court" of The United Methodist Church. Its nine members are elected by the General Conference. The Judicial Council determines the constitutionality of acts or proposed acts of the General, Jurisdictional, Central, and Annual Conferences. It acts on these either on appeal of lower rulings or through requests for declaratory decisions. It also rules on whether acts of other official bodies of the denomination conform to *The Book of Discipline.* This is done in accordance with procedures established in *The Book of Discipline.*

jurisdiction. A large regional division of The United Methodist Church within the United States and composed of the Annual Conferences within its boundaries. These boundaries are determined by the

JURISDICTIONAL CONFERENCE

Constitution. The five jurisdictions are North Central, Northeastern, South Central, Southeastern, and Western.

Jurisdictional Conference. The quadrennial meeting of clergy and lay delegates from the Annual Conferences within its boundaries. The Jurisdictional Conference does the following for the work of the denomination within its boundaries: (1) promotes the evangelistic, educational, missionary, and benevolent interests of the denomination; (2) elects bishops and assigns them to their places of service; (3) establishes such jurisdictional agencies as may be needed; (4) determines the boundaries of its Annual Conferences. All five Jurisdictional Conferences meet once every four years at the same time, as determined by the Council of Bishops.

K

Korean Creed. The statement or affirmation of faith officially adopted when the Korean Methodist Church was organized in 1930. The Korean Creed was prepared as a teaching instrument for occasional use in the Korean churches, and was included in the 1935 and 1966 hymnals of The Methodist Church. A new English translation has been made of the original Korean and is included in *The United Methodist Hymnal* (1989) under the title "A Statement of Faith of the Korean Methodist Church."

kyrie eleison. (ˈkir-ē-ˌä-ə-ˈlä-[ə-]ˌsän) The ancient Greek words meaning "Lord, have mercy." A traditional prayer know as the *Kyrie Eleison* (from its opening words) has been used as a spoken or sung response by worshipers as a response to prayers of confession and as a response used in the service of the Sacrament of the Lord's Supper.

L

laity. Taken from the Greek *laos,* meaning "people." In the Christian church it has meant the people of God. More specifically laity designates those who are not ordained ministers (clergy).

laity, ministry of the.
See *general ministry.*

Laity Sunday. A special Sunday established by the General Conference to be observed on the third Sunday in October. Laity Sunday focuses on the celebration of the ministry of all lay Christians. In many local churches, Laity Sunday is observed by having lay persons lead all parts of the worship service.

The General Board of Discipleship has the responsibility to provide the general supervision and resources for Laity Sunday.

landmarks. Those locations of historical importance to The United Methodist Church on which structures or monuments are in ruins or no longer remain. Had structures remained, these landmarks would qualify as historic shrines. A location is designated a historic landmark by the General Conference upon recommendation of the General Commission on Archives and History.

larger parish. A number of local churches working closely together under a constitution or covenant for the carrying out of their ministry. The larger parish is one form of a cooperative parish and is served by a staff led by a director. The congregations work together through a parish-wide Administrative Council, or Administrative Board and Council on Ministries, and other committees and work groups as needed. Care is taken to see that all the churches are represented on the various working units.

Last Supper, the. The gathering of Jesus and the twelve disciples in the Upper Room on the Thursday of Jesus' final week in Jerusalem. It was in the course of this evening that the final or last supper of Jesus with the disciples was eaten. It is celebrated in the Christian church for the institution of the Sacrament of the Lord's Supper.

See also *Holy Thursday.*

laying on of hands. The placing of hands on the head of an individual in various services to denote the conferring of the Holy Spirit. The laying on of hands is most common in services of baptism, confirmation, ordination, and healing. From the very beginnings of American Methodism, the laying on or imposition of hands by a bishop has been an integral part of the service of ordination of ministers. In more recent years ordained ministers of the Annual Conference and others have been extended the privilege of sharing in this rite of the laying on of hands at ordination. In more recent years also, the receiving of lay persons into the membership of the church has often been symbolized by the laying on of hands by the pastor or pastors of the local church.

lay leader. The local church official, elected by the local church Charge Conference, who serves as the primary lay representative of the members of that local church. The lay leader has a number of specific responsibilities detailed in *The Book of Discipline.*

Districts and Annual Conferences also elect lay leaders to serve as the primary representatives of the lay membership.

layman, laywoman, lay person. Members of The United Methodist Church. They are not ordained ministers (clergy).

See also *laity.*

lay member, Annual Conference. The voting lay delegate to the Annual Conference. Each Annual Conference is required to consist of an equal number of lay members and ministerial members. The vast majority of the lay members of Annual Conferences are elected by pastoral charges to represent them at the sessions of the Annual Conference. In addition, lay persons holding specific lay leadership positions and diaconal ministers are also lay members of the Annual Conference. Lay members may speak and vote on all items coming before the Annual Conference with the exception of those relating to ministerial membership, relationships, ordination, and election of clergy delegates to Jurisdictional and General Conferences.

lay member, local church.
See *membership, local church.*

lay speaker.
See *certified lay speaker.*

leave, study.
See *study leave.*

leave of absence, clergy. The relationship granted (by vote of the ministerial members of an Annual Conference) to those ordained ministers who are temporarily unwilling or unable to carry out the duties of a full-time minister. A leave of absence may be granted to a clergy person because of impaired health, emotional or physical exhaustion, ineffectiveness or incompetence, or other equally sufficient reason. This relationship must be reviewed and approved annually and may not be granted for more than five consecutive years.

lectern. A stand upon which the Bible is placed for reading in a service of worship. The word *lectern* derives from the Latin word *legere,* which means "to read."

lectionary. The list or table of Scripture lessons or passages (lections) to be read in Sunday worship services and on other specific occasions. The term *lectionary* is also used to refer to a book such as *The Common Lectionary,* which contains the listings or tables of passages.

Lent. A forty-day period of focus on penitence and preparation for the Resurrection Event of Easter. Lent begins with Ash Wednesday and ends at sunset Easter Eve. The liturgical color for this season of the Christian year is purple.

license as a local pastor. The approval given to persons not ordained as ministers to preach and conduct worship services and to perform the duties of a pastor under appointment. To obtain a license as a local pastor one must be approved by the district Committee on Ordained Ministry. This approval is given only after the necessary studies for the license have been completed, the individual has been examined by the Committee, and a certificate of good health has been submitted.

litany. A liturgical prayer consisting of a series of invocations and prayer requests. The litany usually consists of sections read alternately by the worship leader and the congregation.

liturgical colors.
See *colors, liturgical.*

local church.
See *church, local.*

local church member.
See *membership, local church.*

local pastor. A lay person approved by the district Committee on Ordained Ministry and licensed by the bishop to perform the duties of a pastor while assigned to a pastoral charge. The authority to serve as a local pastor must be reviewed annually.
See also *license as a local pastor.*

location of clergy. The process by which the authority of a clergy person to exercise the rights and privileges of a minister throughout the denomination is withdrawn. A located minister retains the right to exercise ministerial rights only within the Charge Conference in which his or her membership is held.

The word *location* has a particular meaning in the context of Methodism in the United States. Historically, when a person was judged by the Annual Conference to have the "gifts and graces" to serve effectively as a minister throughout the denomination, that person became a "traveling elder." A traveling elder was one who was considered qualified to serve wherever appointed and thus to become a part of the itinerant or traveling ministry. When a minister was no longer able or willing or judged competent to travel throughout the church, the privilege of traveling was withdrawn and the minister was "located," that is, limited to only one place. The use of the word *location* in the denomination today is based upon this historical usage.

location of clergy, administrative. Removing from the itinerant ministry a ministerial member at the initiative of the Annual Conference. Administrative location is exercised for those ministers who have been unable to perform effectively or competently the duties of the itinerant ministry. These located ministers are limited in the exercise of their ministerial rights to the local church Charge Conference in which they have their membership. Administrative location is voted by the ministerial members of the Annual Conference upon recommendation of the Annual Conference Board of Ordained Ministry.

location of clergy, honorable. The process by which a minister may request to be relieved of the requirement to "travel" or to be a part of the itinerant ministry. Honorable location is granted to ministers in good standing in the Annual Conference. The located minister no longer holds membership in the Annual Conference and becomes a member of a local church. A located minister may exercise ministerial functions only in that local church under the supervision of the pastor. Whether or not to award the status of honorable location is voted on by the ministerial members of the Annual Conference upon recommendation of the Annual Conference Board of Ordained Ministry.

Lord's Day, the. For Christians, the first day of the week, Sunday. Early in the history of the Christian church, Sunday as the first day of the week became a special time of worship, commemorating the Resurrection of Christ.

Lord's Prayer, the. The name generally given to the prayer found in Matthew 6:9-13 and, in a shorter form, in Luke 11:2-4. It is widely used in services of worship and is an important part of the ritual for the Sacrament of the Lord's Supper.

Lord's Supper, Sacrament of the. The traditional name in United Methodism for the Sacrament instituted by Jesus. Over the years the term *Holy Communion* also has become widely accepted as the name for the Sacrament. Eucharist, from the Greek word for thanksgiving, has been yet another traditional name for the Sacrament. "A Service of Word and Table" is the name given for the ritual for this sacrament in *The United Methodist Hymnal* (1989).

This sacrament has been a central and important service throughout the entire life of Methodism. It recalls the Last Supper of Jesus with the disciples. It is a celebration and remembrance of God's grace and mercy in Jesus, of the resurrection of Christ, and of Christ's continuing presence with us. It provides the worshiper with the opportunity to renew the covenant made with God and to be rededicated to service in Christ's name.

Lord's table, the. Another term in United Methodism for the communion table. The term is also used in the following way. In the invitation given by the minister as a part of the Sacrament of the Lord's Supper, people are invited to come to the Lord's table, that is, to participate in the sacrament.

mandatory retirement.
See *retirement, mandatory.*

MARCHA. ('mär-chə) (Metodistas Asociados Representado La Causa De Los Hispano Americanos: Methodists Associated Representing the Cause of Hispanic Americans) A caucus organized to hold the concerns and issues of Hispanic American United Methodists before The United Methodist Church. MARCHA is one of the four caucuses that represent and advocate for racial and ethnic groups within the denomination.
See also *caucus.*

Maundy Thursday.
See *Holy Thursday.*

member, affiliate.
See *affiliate member of a local church (lay); affiliate member of an Annual Conference (ministerial).*

member, Annual Conference lay.
See *lay member, Annual Conference.*

member, associate.

See *associate member of a local church (lay); associate member of an Annual Conference (ministerial)*.

member, local church lay.

See *membership, local church*.

member in full connection, clergy.

See *full connection, minister in*.

membership, Annual Conference. Includes
all clergy members of the Annual Conference and an equal number of lay persons. Lay and ministerial members are determined by different procedures as outlined in *The Book of Discipline*.

See also *lay member, Annual Conference; ministerial member, Annual Conference*.

membership, local church. Includes those persons who have been baptized and who have been received into membership in a local church through confession of faith or by transfer of membership and who have taken the vows of membership. A person who is a member of any local United Methodist church is a member of the United Methodist denomination as a whole. It is the obligation and the responsibility of the pastor of the local church to decide who will be admitted into membership.

membership roll. The permanent record of the membership of a local United Methodist church. The membership roll includes the names and addresses of all baptized persons who have come into membership by confession of faith or by transfer. It includes all members whose names have not been removed

because of death, transfer, withdrawal, or removal for cause.

membership vows. Taken when a person joins a United Methodist church. By taking the membership vows the individual agrees to covenant with God and the members of the local church to keep the vows that are a part of the reception into membership. These vows have four parts: (1) to confess Jesus Christ as Lord and Savior; (2) to believe in the Christian faith as contained in the Old and New Testaments; (3) to promise to live a Christian life; and (4) to uphold The United Methodist Church with one's prayers, presence, gifts, and service.

Methodist, Methodism. Two words, along with Wesleyan, used to describe the movement resulting from the work of John Wesley and his brother Charles. The movement had its very earliest expression in the Holy Club at Oxford. There John and Charles Wesley and others joined together in a highly structured and disciplined pattern of worship, prayer, and study. Those outside the group derisively called the group "Methodists" because of their highly methodical approach to their religion. The name was later applied to the followers of the Wesleys as they actively preached throughout England.

Methodist and Methodism are used to refer to a large family of churches and denominations throughout the world.

Methodist Church, The. Formed in 1939 through the union of The Methodist Episcopal Church, The Methodist Episcopal Church, South, and The Methodist Protestant Church. This union brought together three important streams of American Methodism, which had separated from one another in the first half of the nineteenth century. In 1968 The Methodist Church merged with The Evangelical United Brethren Church to form The United Methodist Church. In its twenty-nine years between 1939 and 1968, The Methodist Church extended its ministry. This was the period of the development of strong and effective general agencies, an increase in the educational standards for clergy, and the outreach of the denomination through its colleges and universities, hospitals and homes.

Methodist Church, The (Great Britain). The name of the present church that embodies the Wesleyan movement in England, Scotland, and Wales. The Methodist Church was formed in 1932 as the result of the merger of three groups: the Wesleyan Methodist Conference or Church (formed in 1791 upon the death of John Wesley), the Primitive Methodist Church (formed in 1811), and the United Methodist Church (formed in 1907). The latter came into being as the result of the union of the Bible Christians (formed in 1815), the Methodist New Connexion (formed in 1797), and the United Methodist Free Churches (formed in 1857). The 1932 union, which formed The Methodist Church, brought together the Wesleyan Methodist Conference with the various groups in Great Britain that had earlier broken away from it. The governing body of The Methodist Church is the Conference, which meets annually. The Conference is presided over by a president, who is elected for a one-year term.

Methodist Episcopal Church, South, The. Formed as the result of the separation from The

Methodist Episcopal Church. Reflecting the debate in the nation over slavery, pastors and members of The Methodist Episcopal Church found themselves embroiled in a strong controversy. At the General Conference of 1844, a Plan of Separation was voted on which would have facilitated an orderly division of the denomination over a period of time, largely along regional or geographic lines. However, the leaders of the southern group immediately set out to establish a separate church. This was done in the first General Conference in 1846 of The Methodist Episcopal Church, South. Though weakened through the period of the Civil War, the new church grew and became a dominant religious force in the southern portion of the nation. In 1939 The Methodist Episcopal Church, South, reunited with The Methodist Episcopal Church and The Methodist Protestant Church to form The Methodist Church.

Methodist Episcopal Church, The. Organized in 1784 at the Christmas Conference in Baltimore, Maryland. Following the independence of the United States, John Wesley believed that American Methodists should establish their own church. To facilitate this Wesley ordained two of his lay preachers and "set apart" Thomas Coke, who was an ordained minister in the Church of England, as a general superintendent and sent the three to assist in the establishment of the new church. He also sent instructions for the new church. The new church under the leadership of Francis Asbury grew rapidly. The Methodist Episcopal Church sent circuit riders throughout the nation and established Annual Conferences as the church matured. In 1808 the first delegated General Conference was held. In 1830, there was a major division over

the issues of the authority of the bishops, the election of the presiding elders (district superintendents), and lay representation in the Annual Conferences, and The Methodist Protestant Church was formed. In 1844 the debate over slavery and the role of bishops led to a break on a geographic basis and The Methodist Episcopal Church, South, was formed. These divisions remained until The Methodist Episcopal Church, The Methodist Episcopal Church, South, and The Methodist Protestant Church united in 1939 to form The Methodist Church.

Methodist Federation for Social Action. An unofficial group within The United Methodist Church that focuses on the promotion of social thought and action in the denomination. The 1908 General Conference gave approval to the formation of this group, then named the Methodist Federation for Social Service. (This same General Conference adopted the first Social Creed.) The Federation attracted strong leadership, and, in the period prior to World War II, it was a strong voice in the denomination and the nation on issues relating to labor legislation, child labor laws, and social reform. Because of its liberal social and economic stances, the Federation was broadly criticized within both the denomination and the nation, and, following World War II, it was accused of communism and communist front activities. In 1952 the General Conference voted for the Federation to remove the word *Methodist* from its name, which it never did, and to affirm that the Federation was not an official agency of the denomination. In 1952 also, the Board of Social and Economic Relations (one of the predecessor boards of the current General Board of Church and Society) was established to carry forward the denomination's official interests in social action and issues. The Methodist Federation for Social Action continues today as an unofficial organization of United Methodists.

Methodist Protestant Church, The. Formed in 1830 as the result of a difference on several issues by a sizable group in The Methodist Episcopal Church. The key issues at dispute were the role of bishops, the desire to elect the presiding elders (district superintendents), and the desire to have lay persons represented in the voting membership of the Annual Conferences. The new denomination soon established its constitution and discipline and held its first General Conference in 1834. In 1939 it united with The Methodist Episcopal Church and The Methodist Episcopal Church, South, to form The United Methodist Church.

military roll. Includes persons in the military services of the United States who are received into the membership of The United Methodist Church. When a person or a family member of a person in military service is received as a member by a chaplain and has no local church to which the membership record may be sent, the chaplain sends this information to the General Board of Discipleship. This Board maintains, on behalf of the denomination, this military roll. As soon as possible these persons are to be transferred to the membership of a local church of their choice.

minimum salary. The smallest amount any minister who is not retired and who is available for full-time appointment to a pastoral charge is entitled to receive from his or her Annual Conference. Each Annual Conference annually establishes the amount of the minimum salary. This is done upon the recommendation of the Annual Conference Commission on Equitable Salaries.

See also *equitable salaries.*

minister. The term which, in its broadest usage in United Methodism, applies to all persons who accept Christ as Savior, who are baptized, and who participate in Christ's ministry of grace through outreach and service in the world. It is the United Methodist conviction that all persons in Christ are called to work for the building up of the church through worship, fellowship, and service to the world.

In a more limited sense, the word *minister* is used to refer to those persons, ordained and diaconal, who serve the church through full-time work. In its most specific usage, minister is used as a synonym for pastor.

minister, diaconal.
See *diaconal minister.*

minister, ordained.
See *ordained minister.*

minister, retired. A ministerial member of an Annual Conference who, because of age, years of service, or other reason, has been placed in the retired relationship by action of the ministerial members of the Annual Conference. This relationship is granted automatically when the minister reaches age seventy.

See also *retirement, mandatory.*

ministerial course of study.
See *course of study.*

Ministerial Education Fund.
Established by the General Conference to support the recruitment and education of ordained and diaconal ministers for United Methodism. The Ministerial Education Fund is one of the general funds of the denomination and is raised through apportionment to the local churches. One quarter of the funds raised remains within the Annual Conference for its program of ministerial and continuing education. The remaining three quarters is primarily distributed to the theological schools of The United Methodist Church for current expenses. A limited portion of the funds is used for ministerial enlistment and development. The Ministerial Education Fund is administered by the General Board of Higher Education and Ministry.

ministerial member, Annual Conference.
A person who has been elected to this status by the ministerial members of the Annual Conference. Each person elected has met the requirements to qualify and has been recommended by the Annual Conference Board of Ordained Ministry. The clergy membership of an Annual Conference consists of all ministerial members in full connection, probational members, associate members, affiliate members, and local pastors under full-time appointment to a pastoral charge.

When a person becomes a member of an Annual Conference, he or she no longer retains membership in a local church.

ministerial support.
The financial underwriting provided for the ministers, ordained and diaconal, of

the denomination. Ministerial support includes salary, provision for housing, pension and disability benefits, and life and health insurance. Each local church is responsible for providing this ministerial support for the ministers appointed to the church. In addition, each local church shares in the responsibility of undergirding the breadth of the ministry of the denomination. As well as supporting its own minister or ministers, it shares in providing minimum salary support for those who qualify, and in the support for the district superintendents and bishops.

minister in the effective relationship. A ministerial member of an Annual Conference who is not retired or on leave of absence. "Effective relationship" means that the ministerial member is available for full-time appointment in the itinerant ministry.

Ministries, Annual Conference Council on. The primary planning and coordinating agency for the program development and implementation of an Annual Conference. The Council on Ministries is to cooperate with the various Annual Conference boards and agencies and to support the local churches in their programs and ministries. The Council reports to and receives its directions from the Annual Conference.

Ministries, General Council on. Established by the General Conference to coordinate and facilitate the program of the denomination as approved by the General Conference. The General Council on Ministries is to encourage, coordinate, and support the general agencies in their respective tasks. The general program agencies are accountable to the Council in

the carrying out of their program. The General Council on Ministries reports to and receives its directions from the General Conference.

Ministries, local church Council on. The primary planning and program organization in the local church. The local church Council on Ministries membership includes the pastor and elected officials representing the program interests and dimensions of the congregation. The Council is amenable to the Administrative Board of the local church.

ministry, general.
See *general ministry.*

ministry, representative.
See *representative ministry.*

minutes of the Conference.
See *Conference Journal.*

mission. In the broadest sense, the entire outreach of the church in worship, witness, and through service. In specific usage in The United Methodist Church, a Mission is the administrative body established for a field of work outside any Annual Conference, Provisional Annual Conference, or Missionary Conference. A Mission is operated under the direction of the General Board of Global Ministries.

missional priority. A response to a critical need in the world that requires a massive and sustained effort of the denomination. A missional priority is established by action of the General Conference upon the recommendation of the General Council on Ministries. A missional priority calls for primary attention to be given to the subject of the priority and for program, budget, and personnel resources to be reordered at every level of the denomination to address the issue.

missionary. A lay or clergy person selected and commissioned to serve in the work of The United Methodist Church or related denominations in other lands or in designated projects in the United States. Missionaries are selected, assigned, and directed in their work by the General Board of Global Ministries.

Missionary Conference. The first step in moving toward becoming an Annual Conference. Because of its particular mission opportunities, its location, or its limited membership and resources, a Missionary Conference does not qualify to be either an Annual Conference or a Provisional Annual Conference. Nonetheless, a Missionary Conference is organized in the same way and with the same rights and powers of an Annual Conference. Administrative guidance and financial support are provided by the General Board of Global Ministries.

missions, local church work area on. The unit in the local church whose purpose is to keep the Council on Ministries or the Administrative Council aware of the purpose and needs of programs and institutions supported by United Methodism in the United States and throughout the world. The work area on missions is to provide resources to be used in study programs on missions and is to relate to and interpret the programs and interests of the General Board of Global Ministries.

133

multiple-charge parish. A number of local churches meeting and working together to serve a geographical area. In a multiple-charge parish, the individual pastoral charges maintain their own identities. They are served by the pastors appointed to the pastoral charges. A director or coordinator for the multiple-charge parish may be appointed. The work of the parish is governed by the parish council in accordance with a constitution or working covenants the parish council devises.

narthex. That portion of a church building between the outside door or other portion of the building and the entrance door to the sanctuary.

National Council of the Churches of Christ in the U.S.A. (NCCC).
The chief ecumenical organization of the Anglican, Old Catholic, Orthodox, and Protestant denominations, which provides services and speaks to important issues. The United Methodist Church is a member of the National Council of the Churches of Christ and through its predecessor denominations has been a member from the beginning of the Council. United Methodists serve as voting members of the governing board, principal divisions, and committees of the Council. Through the Interdenominational Cooperation Fund The United Methodist Church underwrites a share of the financial support for the Council. The offices of the National Council of Churches are in New York City.

National Federation of Asian American United Methodists.
A caucus organized to hold the concerns and issues of Asian American United

Methodists before The United Methodist Church. The National Federation of Asian American United Methodists is one of the four caucuses that represent and advocate for racial and ethnic groups within the denomination.

See also *caucus*.

National Youth Ministry Organization (NYMO).

The youth organization of The United Methodist Church. NYMO has four primary purposes: (1) to advocate for youth with The United Methodist Church; (2) to empower youth as full participants in the life of the church; (3) to be a forum for the expression of youth needs and concerns; and (4) to provide a means of outreach through projects of the Youth Service Fund. The offices of NYMO are in Nashville, Tennessee.

Native American Awareness Sunday.

One of the special Sundays authorized by the General Conference to be observed annually throughout the denomination with an offering. Native American Awareness Sunday is to focus the attention of United Methodists on the gifts and contributions of Native Americans to our society and to our church. The General Council on Ministries determines the Sunday for the observance. Of the funds received in the offering, one half remains within each Annual Conference for the building and strengthening of Native American ministries in the Conference. The remaining one half is to be used by the General Board of Global Ministries to expand the work for Native Americans in target cities in the United States.

Native American International Caucus (NAIC).

A caucus organized to hold the concerns

and issues of Native American United Methodists before The United Methodist Church. The Native American International Caucus is one of the four caucuses that represent and advocate for racial and ethnic groups within the denomination.

See also *caucus.*

nave. The main section of the sanctuary of a church building in which the congregation is seated during worship services. The nave is that area located between the main entrance from the outside or the narthex to the chancel area or railing.

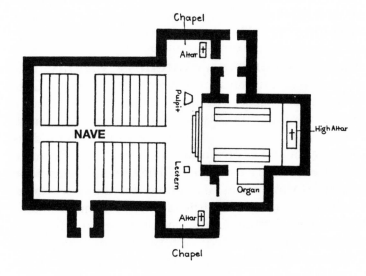

new church, organizing a.
See *organizing a new church.*

Newscope.
A biweekly newsletter of events and happenings in The United Methodist Church. *Newscope* is published by The United Methodist Publishing House and circulates by subscription primarily to pastors and persons in positions of leadership.

New Testament.
Includes the twenty-seven books accepted by Christians as authoritative or canonical concerning the life of Christ and the experience of the early Christian church. Article V of the United Methodist Articles of Religion affirms "All the books of the New Testament, as they are commonly received, we do receive and account canonical." The New Testament serves as the source and guide for our faith in Jesus Christ.

New World Outlook.
A magazine published by the General Board of Global Ministries focusing on issues, concerns, and news of the work of Christian missions throughout the world. Its primary emphasis is upon informing United Methodists of the continuing work of and need for Christian outreach and service.

Nicene Creed.
Frequently used as an affirmation of faith in United Methodist worship services. The Nicene Creed is the historic statement of belief of the Christian faith devised by the Council of Nicaea, convened in A.D. 325 by the Emperor Constantine in the city of Nicaea, located in what is now northwest Turkey. The Creed was revised in 381 by the Council of Constantinople. The Nicene Creed set forth the key affirmations con-

cerning the Christian faith and served as a guide in combating heretical or false teaching. Following the Apostles' Creed, it is the second oldest creed of the Christian faith.

Nominations and Personnel, local church Committee on. Nominates to the Charge Conference officers and members of the Administrative Board or Administrative Council and other committees as required. The Committee on Nominations and Personnel also serves throughout the year to guide the Administrative Board or Administrative Council on personnel matters (other than those involving employed staff) and to recruit, train, and support leaders in the congregation. This Committee is composed of not more than nine persons in addition to the pastor and lay leader. The pastor serves as the chairperson.

offering. The gifts and tithes brought by worshipers to the service. "Offering" is also used to describe the process of collecting or gathering the gifts, as in "taking up the offering." The term *offering* is also commonly used as the name for that portion of the worship service in which the tithes and offerings of those present are received. In United Methodist worship services, there is generally a period of instrumental or choral music while the tithes and gifts are being gathered. It is common practice for the tithes and offerings to be brought to the chancel area of the church and placed on the communion or Lord's table as the congregation stands and sings the Doxology. The pastor then gives a prayer of thanksgiving and dedication of the gifts.

offertory. The choir anthem or other musical selection played or sung while the tithes and offerings are being received from the members of the worshiping congregation.

office. A set form for a service of worship designed for a specific or particular occasion. The office provides the text and the instructions for the service. *The Book of*

Worship (1964) contains eighteen such services under the heading "Occasional Offices of the Church." Among these are "An Office for the Recognition of Church School Officers and Teachers," "An Office for the Organizing of a Church," and "An Office for the Dedication of a Church Building."

older adults. Defined in The United Methodist Church for purposes of program development and organizational representation as all persons sixty-five years of age and older.

Old Testament. The thirty-nine books of the pre-Christian era considered authoritative and canonical by most Protestant churches. Article V of the United Methodist Articles of Religion specifically lists these thirty-nine books. This was done to make clear that other books, such as those in the Apocrypha, were not to be considered part of the Scriptures. The historical position of the Christian church and of United Methodism is that both the Old and New Testaments serve as sources of primary guidance for our faith.

See also *Apocrypha; canon.*

One Great Hour of Sharing. A special Sunday authorized by the General Conference to be observed with an offering taken throughout the denomination on the fourth Sunday of Lent. One Great Hour of Sharing calls United Methodists to share the goodness of life with those in need throughout the world. The offering is to be used for a variety of relief programs. The observance of the Sunday is under the general direction of United Methodist Communications. The funds are administered by the United Methodist Committee on Relief Department, General Board of Global Ministries.

ordained minister. A person, in the traditional language of United Methodism, "within the ministry of the baptized who is called of God and set aside by the Church for the specialized ministry of Word, Sacrament, and Order." To qualify for ordination an individual must meet the requirements for membership set forth by The United Methodist Church and the Annual Conference and must have completed the necessary educational training. The individual must also receive the recommendation of the Annual Conference Board of Ordained Ministry and the affirmative vote of the ministerial members of the Conference to receive ordination as a deacon or an elder. Following ordination one has the authority to exercise the responsibilities and duties of an ordained minister.

order (organization). Refers to organizational patterns of United Methodism. The word *order* refers to the way The United Methodist Church organizes and structures its corporate life to accomplish its mission in the world.

order (persons). A term in only limited use today used to distinguish between groups or categories of persons in the denomination. For example, in Annual Conferences and the General Conference, it is possible, though rarely done, for the lay and clergy delegates to vote separately. This is known as voting by "orders." In The United Methodist Church there are two levels or orders of ministerial ordination, deacon and elder.

Ordinal, the. The official text of the ritual used for the services of ordination of deacons and elders and for the consecration of bishops.

ordination. The act of conferring ministerial orders. Ordination is performed by a bishop. The central portion of the ceremony is the words granting the authority of the order of deacon or elder and the laying on of hands by the bishop and others on the person being ordained. Through ordination The United Methodist Church grants the person the approval of the denomination to serve as an ordained minister, and the authority to carry out those acts specifically reserved to the clergy.

organizing a new church. Procedures prescribed by *The Book of Discipline* for the starting of a new church. The district superintendent or a designated pastor meets with those interested in organizing a new church. Those desiring to join are formally taken into the membership of the new congregation. A Constituting Church Conference is then called by the district superintendent to establish the structure for the church, and a pastor is appointed. The bishop must approve the formation of the new church, and the location for the church must be approved by the district Board of Church Location and Building.

Otterbein, Philip William. Founder of The Church of the United Brethren in Christ, one of the predecessor branches of The United Methodist Church. Otterbein (1726–1813), a native of Germany, was ordained in the German Reformed Church. He came to the United States in 1752 and served as the pastor of Reformed congregations in Pennsylvania and Maryland. In 1774 he became the pastor of an independent Reformed congregation in Baltimore, Maryland, which he served until his death. He had close ties with the American Methodists and assisted in the ordination of

Francis Asbury at the Methodist Christmas Conference of 1784. Otterbein became a leader of a small group within the Reformed Church seeking to promote a spirit of inward piety. In 1800 The Church of the United Brethren in Christ was formed. Otterbein along with Martin Boehm was elected bishop. The relationships between the leaders of this church and The Methodist Episcopal Church were close. The Church of the United Brethren in Christ merged with The Evangelical Association in 1946 to form The Evangelical United Brethren Church. In 1968 The Evangelical United Brethren Church merged with The Methodist Church to form The United Methodist Church.

 **P**

pall. The cloth covering placed over a casket during a funeral. When a pall is used, flowers are not placed on the casket.

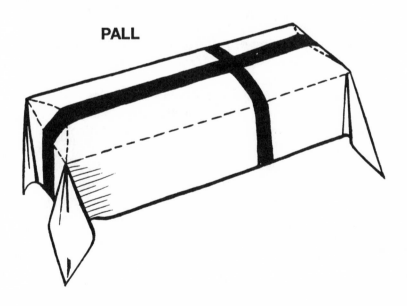

PALL

pallbearers. Those persons who carry the casket in the course of a funeral. In some funerals, additional persons, who do not carry the casket, are named honorary pallbearers.

palms. The leaves of the palm tree used in many churches as a part of the procession and the observances of the Palm Sunday worship services. The palms symbolize the response of the people to the entry of Jesus into Jerusalem at the beginning of Holy Week. They are burned before the following Ash Wednesday, their remains becoming the ashes.

Palm Sunday (Passion Sunday). The Sunday immediately preceding Easter Sunday. Palm Sunday commemorates the entry of Jesus into Jerusalem and begins the series of observances focusing on the events of Holy Week. This Sunday is also often referred to as Passion Sunday, marking the beginning of the passion or suffering of Jesus leading to and including the crucifixion.

paraments. The linens and cloth hangings used on communion tables, altars, pulpits, and lecterns. The colors of the paraments reflect the traditional colors of the seasons of the Christian year. The paraments are changed as the seasons of the Christian year change. Often the paraments are embellished with specific symbols appropriate to the Christian season. In many United Methodist churches, an altar guild of lay volunteers is responsible for the care and changing of the paraments.

parish. The area served by the local church. Parish also tends to be used often as a synonym for the local church and the people it serves. United Methodism does not use the term, as some denominations do, to mean a clearly designated geographical area from which persons are expected to attend a specific local church.

The word *parish* is used in one specific sense by United Methodism in describing and identifying procedures related to cooperative parish ministries and the Annual Conference Committee on Parish and Community Development. In this context parish means the area of service ministered to by one or more churches.

parsonage. Owned by the pastoral charge, the house provided as the residence for the family of a pastor. A housing allowance may be granted by the pastoral charge for the minister in lieu of a parsonage, provided this is done in compliance with Annual Conference policy.

Paschal candle. The large candle placed near the Lord's table and lighted during the Easter season, placed near the baptismal font at other seasons and lighted for baptisms, and placed lighted near the head of the coffin at church funerals.

Passion Sunday.
See *Palm Sunday.*

pastor. The ordained or licensed person who has been appointed by the bishop to be in charge of a local church or churches.

The pastor in this formal sense is the official representative of the Annual Conference and is responsible for serving effectively in the ministry of "Word, Sacrament, and Order" in that appointment. In a less formal sense, pastor is a title synonymous with minister.

pastoral charge. One or more local United Methodist churches to which an ordained or licensed minister is appointed by the bishop. The pastoral charge is organized according to *The Book of Discipline* and has a Charge Conference.

pastoral letter. An open letter sent to the local churches and members by a bishop of the church. From time to time, the Council of Bishops of The United Methodist Church has issued a pastoral letter on a matter of great importance. This is sent throughout the church with the request that it be read and studied in all local churches. Individual bishops may send a pastoral letter for the churches in the Annual Conference or Conferences of their episcopal area.

pastoral ministry. The active service of an ordained minister as a pastor in local churches. Pastoral ministry does not refer to other types of ministries such as military or civilian chaplaincies, missions, teaching, or administration.

pastoral prayer. The prayer offered by the minister in the course of a service of worship for and on behalf of the congregation. Traditionally, the pastoral prayer has occupied a prominent place in the period of prayers in the Sunday worship service.

Pastor-Parish Relations, local church Committee on. Or Staff-Parish Relations Committee. It works closely with the pastor and the staff concerning their relationship with the congregation and the entire work of the church. This committee is in essence the personnel committee of the pastoral charge. The committee is to be sensitive to the opinions and concerns of the congregation concerning the pastor and staff. It is to confer with the district superintendent or the bishop concerning the appointment of the pastor for the church. The committee recommends the salary for the pastor to the Charge Conference. It consists of from five to nine members of the pastoral charge.

pastors' schools. Continuing education events for ministers of an Annual Conference or an area. The pattern for pastors' schools is more varied than in former times. Traditionally, the pastors' schools consisted of a one-week period of time in which the ministers of a conference gathered to engage in study, renewal, and fellowship. The week would contain worship, including sermons by a guest preacher, lectures, and small-group study and sharing.

Peace, the. The ancient and traditional practice of Christians greeting one another with a sign or word of love and blessing. This is done with an embrace, a handshake, a handclasp, or the exchange of a word of blessing. This practice has been revived in recent years in United Methodist and other Christian churches.

Peace with Justice Sunday. A special Sunday authorized by the General Conference to be observed with an offering to be taken up throughout the denomination on the second Sunday after Pentecost. The focus of the observance is on a witness to God's demand for a faithful, just, disarmed, and secure world. Of the monies received, one half remains in the Annual Conference for Peace with Justice projects. The other half goes to the General Board of Church and Society for its program of Peace with Justice ministries. The General Board of Church and Society is responsible for the general supervision of the observance of this special Sunday.

Pensions, General Board of. The agency established by the General Conference to provide the general supervision and administration of the pension and benefit programs, plans, and funds of The United Methodist Church. The General Board of Pensions administers and disburses the retirement and benefit funds of the various Annual Conferences. It works closely with the Board of Pensions of each Annual Conference. The offices of the General Board of Pensions are in Evanston, Illinois.

Pentecost. One of the principal days of the Christian year, celebrated on the fiftieth day after Easter. The Greek word *pentecoste* means "fiftieth day." Pentecost is the day on which the Christian church commemorates the coming of the Holy Spirit upon the apostles and others assembled in Jerusalem. It marks the beginning of the Christian church and the proclamation of its message throughout the world and is often referred to as the birthday of the church. The liturgical color for Pentecost is red.

Traditionally, Pentecost has been a day for baptisms. Because it was the custom in the early church for persons being baptized to wear white robes or clothing, the day also came to be known as Whitsunday, a contraction of white Sunday.

Pentecost, Season After. The period in the Christian calendar extending from the day after Pentecost Sunday to the first Sunday in Advent. By tradition, the Sundays after Pentecost are numbered. The first Sunday after Pentecost is Trinity Sunday, for which the liturgical color is white. The last Sunday in this period is Christ the King Sunday, for which the color is also white. The color for the rest of the Season After Pentecost is green. This season focuses on the significance of the church as a sign of God's continuing presence and activity in the world.

petition. In the broadest sense, an earnest request, prayer, or supplication to God. Often such petitions are intercessory prayers, lifting the concerns for an individual or a group of people to God.

petitions to General Conference. A request to the General Conference for official action on a topic or issue. A petition to the General Conference may be a request for an amendment to the Constitution, a change in the legislative content of *The Book of Discipline*, an approval of a resolution, or an approval of a report. Any official organization (local churches, Annual Conferences, general agencies), lay member, or ordained minister of The United Methodist Church has the right to send a petition to the General Conference. Formerly, petitions to the General Conference were known as Memorials.

Some Annual Conferences use the petition format for bringing items to the Annual Conference for consideration and action.

petitions to Judicial Council. Requests to the Judicial Council to make declaratory rulings and decisions. Upon petition, the Judicial Council rules on the constitutionality and legality of actions of the

151

General, Jurisdictional, Central, and Annual Conferences. The Judicial Council also rules, upon petition,
on decisions made by presiding bishops and on matters advancing on appeal from lower tribunals in matters of church trials. A petition to the Judicial Council
may be made by the General Conference, a Jurisdictional, Central, or Annual Conference, the Council of
Bishops, or a general agency on issues directly pertaining to them. An individual lay person or minister
or a local church may not petition the Judicial Council
for a ruling.

pew. A long bench used for the seating of worshipers in churches. The current usage of the word
pew derives from the enclosed space or compartment
in a church in which benches or seats were provided
for a family and for which a pewage or pew rental
was required.

postlude. The musical selection played or sung at
the conclusion of a service of worship. The postlude
generally follows a benediction given by the pastor or
other worship leader.

prayer desk, prayer bench, or prie-Dieu.
([']prē-'dyə[r]) A small kneeling bench designed to be
used by a person at prayer. The prie-Dieu (which in
French means literally "pray God") is often built with a
raised shelf on which the elbows or a book may be
placed. Many a prie-Dieu is small and designed for private devotions. Local churches often have a prie-Dieu
for use in services. Examples of this include the prayer
benches used by the clergy during communion services
or the prayer bench used by a wedding couple in the
course of a marriage service.

Prayer of Consecration.
See *Great Thanksgiving, the.*

prelude. The musical selection played or sung at the beginning of a service of worship. It is generally considered a part of the gathering time of the congregation for the worship service.

preparatory member. A person who is in preparation for full membership in the local church. This includes persons who have declared their interest in the local church or who have enrolled in classes in preparation for taking the membership vows.

In The United Methodist Church, the term *preparatory member* is defined specifically to mean all baptized children and youth eighteen years of age and younger who are not yet members of the local church.

Preparatory Membership Roll.
Contains the names and addresses and other pertinent information of all baptized children and youth eighteen years of age and younger who are not full members of the local church. If a youth does not become a full member by age nineteen, the name is to be transferred to the Constituency Roll. The Preparatory Membership Roll is also to include the names of other persons who are enrolled in confirmation preparation. Each local church is to maintain a current Preparatory Membership Roll.

presiding elder. A historical term in American Methodism for an elder who supervised a number of pastoral charges. As Methodism in America grew and geographically defined districts were established, the office of presiding elder was established to oversee the work of the local churches within a district. In 1939, when the three Methodist denominations united to form The Methodist Church, the use of this title was discontinued. It was replaced with the title *district superintendent.*

probationary member, Annual Conference, (ministerial). A person who has met all of the conditions set forth in *The Book of Discipline* for probationary membership and has been received by vote of the ministerial members of the Annual Conference. The probationary membership period is considered a trial period leading to full ministerial membership in the Annual Conference. During this period, probationary members complete their education and training, serve as pastors, and are evaluated as to their readiness and fitness for ministry. Probationary members may be ordained as deacons but not as elders.

program year. The schedule on which program planning is carried out in The United Methodist Church. The program year is the same as the calendar year (January 1 through December 31).

Provisional Annual Conference. A Conference that, because of its limited lay and ministerial membership, does not qualify for Annual Conference status. A Provisional Annual Conference must have at least ten ministerial members and be growing in numerical and financial strength. It is organized like an Annual Conference and has the same powers and functions, subject to the approval of the presiding bishop.

psalm. The Hebrew name given to hymns or songs of praise. Although there are many other psalms in

Hebrew literature, for ancient Israel the collection of the 150 became their hymnal.

For Christians the term *psalm* refers only to the 150 psalms composing the book of Psalms of the Old Testament. Christians have used the psalms through the centuries as a way to express their faith and as a resource for personal prayer and devotional life.

psalter. A separate book or portion of a book or hymnal containing the Psalms. The psalter often contains the Psalms arranged for singing or liturgical or devotional use. *The United Methodist Hymnal* (1989) includes a psalter of 100 psalms selected for public worship.

Publication, General Board of.
See *United Methodist Publishing House, The.*

pulpit. A stand or tall reading desk used by the minister for preaching or for conducting a service of worship. In most United Methodist churches the pulpit is on a dais.

quadrennium. A period of four years. The quadrennium is the basic planning period for the denomination level of The United Methodist Church. The General Conference meets only once every four years. It revises *The Book of Discipline,* approves important program emphases, and establishes the budget for the next four years. The general agencies work on the same four-year program and funding cycle. Officially, the four-year quadrennium begins on January 1 following the adjournment of the General Conference.

Quarterly Conference. The historical name used for the meeting of the district superintendent with the leadership of a pastoral charge. In 1968 the name of this meeting was changed to Charge Conference. The term *Quarterly Conference* grew out of the fact that, for Methodism's first century and beyond, it was the responsibility of the presiding elder to visit each pastoral charge four times a year. At this time the presiding elder, now called the district superintendent, conducted official business of the charge. The presiding elder also received a portion of his salary as well as the church's contribution to the denomination's budget.

This came to be known as "the quarterage." In this century, the Quarterly Conference came to be held less frequently, finally only annually.

Quarterly Review. A journal containing scholarly articles on theology and other topics of academic interest. It is published four times a year by the General Board of Higher Education and Ministry.

Questions, Wesley's Historic. The set of questions devised by John Wesley to be asked of persons presenting themselves as candidates for the ministry. These questions were first asked by John Wesley in 1746 at the third conference of Methodist preachers in England. They were the standards by which prospective preachers have been judged through the years. Wesley's questions remain an integral part of the process leading to Annual Conference membership and ordination.

R

reaffirmation of faith. The public reaffirmation of the baptismal vows by persons who have previously affirmed them either at the time of baptism or at confirmation. Reaffirmation of faith is most frequent when an individual is joining a local church.

reaffirmation of the baptismal covenant. The remembrance of the baptismal experience and the vows taken at that time. The reaffirmation of the baptismal covenant is held during a worship service. It focuses on God's grace extended through baptism and the response of the individual for faithful Christian living. An order for a service for the congregational reaffirmation of the baptismal covenant has been included in *The United Methodist Hymnal* (1989).

Religion and Race, General Commission on. An agency established by the General Conference whose primary task is to focus on bringing about full and equal participation of the racial and ethnic constituencies in the life of The United Methodist Church. The Commission is to work with the general agencies, institutions, and structures of the denomination to ensure that full participation is achieved. The Commission carries out its work through advocacy of the issues and by reviewing and monitoring the practices of the denomination. The offices of the General Commission on Religion and Race are located in Washington, D.C.

The Book of Discipline also makes provision for a Commission on Religion and Race to be established in each Annual Conference to address these same purposes and issues.

Religion and Race, local church work area on.
Serves to keep the local church Council on Ministries or the Administrative Council aware of the meaning and content of the racial and ethnic issues within The United Methodist Church. The local church work area on Religion and Race is to recommend program opportunities for worship, fellowship, witness, study, nurture, and service with the full range of racial and ethnic persons, groups, and congregations.

removal by Charge Conference action.
Action taken by the local church Charge Conference to remove a person from the membership of a local church. This action can be taken if the member resides in the community but is no longer active in the life of the church, the member resides outside the community and is not active in any church, or the address of the member is unknown. Removal by Charge Conference action is done on the recommendation of the pastor and the local church work area on evangelism or Commission on Evangelism. Final action can be taken only after the member's name has been listed with the Charge Conference for three consecutive years.

reports to the Charge Conference.
Those reports brought to the Charge Conference which review and eval-

uate the performance of the various aspects of the life of the local church. The Charge Conference is to receive reports from all of the committees, work areas, and organizations of the congregation. These various reports become a part of the complete report of the Charge Conference to the district superintendent.

representative ministry. The ministry of those persons who have been called to the full-time ministry and meet the qualifications established for this ministry. Those called to the representative ministry serve to strengthen and enhance the general ministry of all believers. The representative ministry includes ordained and diaconal ministers who are affirmed in their call through ordination or consecration by the Annual Conference.

reredos. ('rer-ə-ˌdäs) An ornamental screen or wall located behind the communion table or altar. Some-

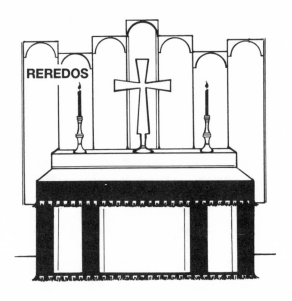

times the reredos consists of a wooden or stone carving, often quite elaborate and detailed.

Resolutions, The Book of. The volume containing the text of all resolutions or pronouncements on issues approved by the General Conference and currently valid. *The Book of Resolutions* contains not only the resolutions and policy statements passed by the most recent General Conference, but also all such statements still considered to represent the position of The United Methodist Church. The text of any resolution is considered the official position of the denomination on that subject.

response. The answering or completing by the congregation of a declaration or statement by the pastor or leader in a service of worship. A response may be said or sung, as in the response in a liturgical use of the Psalms. A response is the second portion of a responsive reading or the second half of a versicle.

Response. A magazine focusing on news, articles, and program resources for the United Methodist Women groups. *Response* is published by the Women's Division of the General Board of Global Ministries.

Restrictive Rules, the. Statements specifying six things the General Conference of The United Methodist Church may not do. The Restrictive Rules are found in Section III of the Constitution. The General Conference may not "revoke, alter, or change" the Articles of Religion, the Confession of Faith, or the General Rules of the Societies. The General Conference may not do away with the episcopacy or the right of ministers to trial or appeal. Further, the General Conference may not appropriate the net income of the Publishing House for any purpose other than clergy pensions.

The Restrictive Rules were established by the General Conference of 1808, which voted that the General Conference would have broad authority over the denomination except for those items protected by what are now called the Restrictive Rules. Through the years the Restrictive Rules have been modified only slightly through the constitutional amendment process.

retired minister.

See *minister, retired.*

retirement, involuntary.
The process by which an Annual Conference may retire any ministerial members with or without their consent and irrespective of age. Involuntary retirement can be effected only upon the approval of two-thirds of the ministerial members upon recommendation of the Board of Ordained Ministry and the Cabinet.

retirement, mandatory.
The process which requires the retirement of ordained and diaconal ministers when they have reached age seventy on or before July 1.

The mandatory retirement date for bishops is more difficult to describe inasmuch as they are assigned for four-year appointments to their episcopal areas. A bishop must retire on August 31 following the regular session of the Jurisdictional Conference if the bishop's sixty-sixth birthday occurred on or before July 1 of the year in which the Jurisdictional Conference was held. The effect of this ruling is to require all bishops to retire on or before age seventy.

retirement, ministers in. Those ministers who have been placed in the retired membership relationship in the Annual Conference. They are retired either at their own request or by action of the ministerial members of the Annual Conference. As a retired member, the minister is relieved of the obligation to receive an appointment to a pastoral charge. Normal retirement may come when the minister reaches age sixty-five or has completed forty years of service. Under specific circumstances, a minister may retire earlier by action of the Annual Conference. Mandatory retirement comes at age seventy.

See also *retirement, mandatory.*

retreat. A period of time spent away from the regular routine. A retreat is often used for study and spiritual growth, either by an individual or by members of a group. Retreats are also used by members and staff of local churches and conference and general agencies for program and administrative planning.

Reverend, The. The accepted ascription of respect in English for a clergy person. When the ascription is written, the word *Reverend* is an adjective and must be followed by the noun modified. Therefore, the definite article *The* should always precede the word *Reverend,* which is then followed by the appropriate title and name, such as The Reverend Mr. Smith or The Reverend John Smith.

ring, wedding.
See *wedding ring.*

ritual. A specific form including text for the conducting of a service. Usually, the ritual has been established by custom and tradition.

Ritual, The. The phrase used historically in United Methodism to refer to those services and offices used by ministers and congregations for conducting the formal services of the denomination. The earliest forms of these services came to American Methodism from John Wesley's Prayer Book. In their early form they were included in the 1792 *Discipline* and became known as *The Ritual*. These services or offices included the Lord's Supper or Holy Communion; Infant Baptism; Adult Baptism; Matrimony; Burial of the Dead; Ordination of Deacons and Elders; and the Consecration of Bishops. In the early 1870s, an order of service, Confirmation and the Reception of Members, was added.

Since 1964 considerable research and study, especially in the light of the union of The Evangelical United Brethren Church and The Methodist Church in 1968, has been conducted on these services. The 1984 General Conference approved a set of General Services, which had been devised for The United Methodist Church and added to the Ritual for the denomination. As a consequence, the Ritual of The United Methodist Church consists of those services contained in *The Ritual of The Evangelical United Brethren Church* (1959), "The General Services of the Church" in *The Book of Worship* (1964) of The Methodist Church, *The Ordinal* (1981), and "The General Services of the Church" (1984).

rolls, membership. Those records each local church is required to maintain on the membership. The various membership rolls are:

1) Affiliate Membership Roll
2) Associate Membership Roll

164

3) Constituency Roll
4) Full Membership Roll
5) Members Removed by Charge Conference Action
6) Preparatory Membership Roll

rubrics. The directions or rules given for the proper conduct of worship rituals and services. The word *rubrics* comes from the Latin word for red. The instructions or directions are called rubrics because at one time these instructions were printed almost universally in red. This was done to provide a contrast with the black print of the content of the services. This practice is followed in many of the publications of The United Methodist Church including *The United Methodist Hymnal* (1989).

The word *rubrics* is also sometimes used to refer to the *Discipline*'s rules and procedures, which must be followed in carrying out the work of the denomination.

Rural Life Sunday. An annual observance authorized by the General Conference to be carried out on a date determined by each Annual Conference. Rural Life Sunday is to be observed without a special offering being taken. The primary focus of the observance is to celebrate the rural roots and heritage of The United Methodist Church and to affirm the people and communities worldwide who work and live on the land. The observance of Rural Life Sunday is under the general supervision of the General Board of Global Ministries.

S

sabbatical leave. A period of time granted to ordained and diaconal ministers for a program of study and travel. The term sabbatical comes from the Hebrew word for rest. The sabbath day was the seventh day and was to be revered because God rested on the seventh day. The sabbatical year or seventh year was observed in ancient Judea as a time to allow the fields to lie fallow. Thus the concept of a leave every seventh year for rest and study developed.

In The United Methodist Church a minister is eligible for a sabbatical leave after having served six consecutive years or more in a full-time appointment. The normal length of time for a leave is one year. A bishop may be granted a sabbatical leave for one year after having served as a bishop for at least two quadrenniums.

sacrament. A religious ceremony considered especially sacred because of God's acting through the sacrament or because it is a sign or symbol of a significant reality. The United Methodist understanding of the sacraments is informed by the sixteenth Article of Religion. It states: "Sacraments ordained of Christ are not only badges or tokens of Christian men's profession, but rather they are certain signs of grace, and God's good will toward us, by which he doth work invisibly in us, and doth not only quicken, but also strengthen and confirm, our faith in him." The United Methodist Church recognizes only two sacraments: Baptism and the Lord's Supper.

Sacrament of Baptism.
See *Baptism, Sacrament of.*

Sacrament of the Lord's Supper.
See *Lord's Supper, Sacrament of the.*

sacristy. The room, generally located immediately at the front of a church sanctuary, often just off the chancel area, where the paraments, communion ware, and

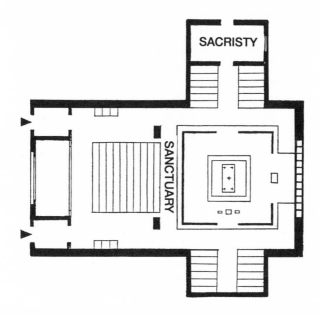

other materials for the communion table and chancel area are kept. The sacristy in some United Methodist churches is also the room in which the bread and wine are prepared for the Sacrament of the Lord's Supper.

sanctuary. The main worship room or auditorium in a United Methodist church building. The sanctuary for United Methodism includes the nave, chancel, and choir areas.

Sanctus. ('saŋ[k]-təs) An ancient hymn of adoration beginning with the words, "Holy, holy, holy," and used as part of the Sacrament of the Lord's Supper. *Sanctus* is the Latin word for holy.

schools of mission. Short-term schools operated under the auspices of the Women's Division of the General Board of Global Ministries. The schools of mission are generally held for one-week periods in the summer months in Annual Conferences throughout the United States. The primary purpose of the schools of mission is to provide information and train leaders in the approved studies on mission fields and concerns.

schools of theology. Institutions of The United Methodist Church established for the primary purpose of educating persons to serve effectively as ordained and diaconal ministers. The schools of theology are also to engage in research and studies for the clarification and interpretation of the Christian faith. There are thirteen United Methodist schools of theology, all training ministers at the graduate level. In addition to their own sources of support, the schools of theology receive financial support for current operating expenses from the Ministerial Education Fund.

Scripture lesson. A designated passage of the Bible read in the course of a service of worship. Often, United Methodist worship services include a Scripture lesson or reading from the Old Testament and from the New Testament Gospels or Epistles or both.

secretary, Annual Conference. The person elected to be responsible for the proper development and maintenance of the records of the Annual Conference. The secretary of the Annual Conference is responsible for maintaining the official record of the daily proceedings or minutes of the Annual Conference sessions, compiling and publishing the journal, and keeping records pertaining to ministerial trials, records of official certificates and credentials, and other specified documents and records. The secretary is elected by the Annual Conference and is usually an ordained minister.

secretary, General Conference. The person elected by the General Conference to be responsible for the proper development of all the official records of the General Conference. The secretary of the General Conference is responsible for maintaining the official record of the daily proceedings, for collecting and processing the petitions submitted, for the appropriate referencing of the petitions to the legislative committees, and for a variety of other matters relating to the functioning of the General Conference. During the course of the General Conference, a secretary-designate is elected to serve the next General Conference. To do this, a nomination is presented by the Council of Bishops to the Conference, and other nominations may be made by General Conference members.

seminary.
See *schools of theology*.

shrine. A building linked with significant events or outstanding personalities or both in the origin and development of The United Methodist Church. A historic shrine is so designated because it is considered to have distinct historic value and interest for the denomination as a whole. A building is designated a historic shrine by action of the General Conference upon the recommendation of the General Commission on Archives and History.

site. A location or building judged by the Jurisdictional or Annual Conference presiding over it to be of historical significance for its connection with events or personalities involved in the development of United Methodism. The General Commission on Archives and History maintains a register of all historic sites.

sixteen-year rule. The regulation stating that any person, lay or clergy, who has been a voting member of general agencies for four consecutive quadrenniums (sixteen years) is to be ineligible for election to the membership of a general agency in the succeeding quadrennium. The sixteen-year rule was approved by the General Conference in 1984 and does not apply to bishops.

Social Creed, the. A set of affirmations concerning United Methodist beliefs about the relationship of the church to the social issues and the world. The Social Creed is approved by the General Conference as a part of a larger document, the Social Principles, and the action of the General Conference recommends that the

Social Creed be used frequently in Sunday worship services. The first Social Creed was adopted by the 1908 General Conference of The Methodist Episcopal Church. The Social Creed has been reviewed and revised through the years by the General Conference, and is printed in *The Book of Discipline.*

Social Principles, the. A lengthy document setting forth the basic position of The United Methodist Church on important social issues. The Social Principles represent the effort of the General Conference to speak to human issues in the contemporary world from a sound biblical and theological foundation. The Social Principles document is reviewed by each General Conference and is printed in full in *The Book of Discipline.*

Speaking for The United Methodist Church. The provision enacted by the General Conference that establishes clearly how the positions of The United Methodist Church are to be given. This regulation in *The Book of Discipline* states: "No person, no paper, no organization, has the authority to speak officially for The United Methodist Church, this right having been reserved exclusively to the General Conference under the Constitution. Any written public policy statement issued by a general church agency shall clearly identify either at the beginning or at the end that the statement represents the position of that general agency and not necessarily the position of The United Methodist Church. Any individual member called to testify before a legislative body to represent The United Methodist Church shall be allowed to do so only by reading, without elaboration, the resolutions and positions adopted by the General Conference of The United Methodist Church."

special appointment.

See *appointment beyond the local church.*

special days (Sundays).

Those Sundays authorized by the General Conference to be set aside for a denomination-wide emphasis. The General Conference has approved special Sundays to be observed both with an offering and without an offering. (Each of these special Sundays is described elsewhere in this dictionary.) Those special Sundays approved which include an offering are: (1) Human Relations Day, (2) One Great Hour of Sharing, (3) World Communion Sunday, (4) United Methodist Student Day, (5) Peace with Justice Sunday, and (6) Native American Awareness Sunday. Those without an offering are: (1) Heritage Sunday, (2) Laity Sunday, and (3) Rural Life Sunday. In addition, the General Conference has authorized two special Sundays with offerings that may be observed at the discretion and timing of the Annual Conference: (1) Christian Education Sunday and (2) Golden Cross Sunday.

Standard Sermons of John Wesley, the.

Forty-four sermons of Wesley published in the first four volumes of his sermons. The Standard Sermons set forth those doctrines Wesley embraced and taught "as essentials of true religion." These sermons, along with Wesley's *Notes upon the New Testament,* were commended to preachers. They have continued to be standard reference points for the understanding of Wesleyan theology.

station.

A pastoral charge comprising only one local church. This is in contrast to a circuit, which contains two or more local churches.

Status and Role of Women, General Commission on the.

An agency established by the General Conference in 1972 whose primary task is to challenge The United Methodist Church to a commitment to the full participation of women in the complete life and mission of the church. In fulfilling this task, the Commission serves as an advocate for and on behalf of women, seeks to eliminate inequities in relation to women in the church, and monitors the general agencies, institutions, and connectional structures to ensure inclusiveness of women. The offices of the General Commission on the Status and Role of Women are in Evanston, Illinois. *The Book of Discipline* also provides for the establishment of a Commission on the Status and Role of Women in each Annual Conference to address these same purposes and issues.

status and role of women, local church work area on the.

The work area that keeps the local church Council on Ministries or the Administrative Council aware of the meaning of the continuing commitment of United Methodists to the full and equal participation of women in the complete life and mission of the church. The work area is to provide programs and opportunities for local church members to work on these issues. The chairperson of the work area is to be a woman.

stewardship, local church work area on.

The work area in the local church that is to interpret and encourage stewardship in the local church. The work area on stewardship encourages tithing as the minimum standard of giving, and works with the Council on Ministries or the Administrative Council to devise plans and programs to encourage the growth of stewardship in the local church.

stole. A long narrow strip of material worn by ordained and diaconal ministers. Deacons and diaconal ministers by custom wear the stole over the left shoulder only. Ordained elders, including bishops, wear the stole around the neck over both shoulders. The stole worn in a service of worship is usually of the appropriate color for the day or season of the Christian calendar. Often stoles are decorated, especially with Christian symbols appropriate to the Christian day or season.

STOLE

Student Day.
See *United Methodist Student Day.*

Student Loan Fund.
See *United Methodist Student Loan Fund.*

study leave. A period of time granted to ministers for study and continuing education. Annual Conferences urge pastors to maintain a program of continuing education. Most recommend that the program allow for at least one week each year and at least one full month each quadrennium for study. An ordained minister may also request an educational leave of up to six months while holding a pastoral appointment.

See also *sabbatical leave.*

Sunday school. The name traditionally given to the teaching activities taking place in the local church on Sunday morning, either before or after the worship service.

See also *church school.*

superintendency. Residing in the office of the bishop and extending to the district superintendent, the task of overseeing the work of The United Methodist Church. Those who superintend carry primary responsibility for ordering the life of the church. The superintendency is to enable the church to be effective in worship and outreach and in its program and organizational life as a whole. A method for carrying this out is in the careful deployment of ministers to local churches through the appointment process. *The Book of Discipline* states: "The formal leadership in The United Methodist Church, located in these superintending offices, is an integral part of the system of an itinerant ministry."

superintendent, district.
See *district superintendent.*

superintendent, general.
See *bishop.*

175

surplice. A loose white vestment with large open sleeves that generally extends to the knees in length. The surplice is usually worn as an outer garment over a cassock. It is sometimes worn in United Methodist services by acolytes or choirs, more rarely by pastors.

SURPLICE ____

surrender of credentials. The procedure whereby local pastors or ordained ministers return their credentials upon leaving the ministry. When local pastors or ordained ministers decide to leave the ministry and withdraw, they must surrender the credentials given to them by the Annual Conference. The credentials are to be surrendered to the district superintendent and deposited with the Conference secretary.

Sursum Corda. (ˌsú[ə]r-səm-'kȯrd-ə) The versicle and response traditionally a part of the ritual for the Sacrament of the Lord's Supper. *Sursum Corda* is Latin for "Lift Up Your Hearts."

T

table, the Lord's.
See *Lord's table, the*.

Tenebrae. ('ten-ə-,brā) One of the special worship services of Holy Week. The word *tenebrae* is Latin for darkness. The distinguishing feature of Tenebrae is the gradual extinguishing of candles and lights following the reading of Scripture passages until the sanctuary is in darkness. The service focuses on the passion and death of Jesus and is generally observed on Good Friday evening, but it may also be used as a closing portion of the Holy Thursday service.

termination of Annual Conference membership (ministerial).
The removal of a minister's membership in an Annual Conference and as a consequence the withdrawal of the authority to function as an ordained minister of The United Methodist Church. Annual Conference membership may be terminated by honorable location (allowing the pastor to function only in his or her local church), administrative location, surrender of the ministerial office, withdrawal to unite with another denomination, or withdrawal under complaints or charges. The granting of honorable or administrative location must be voted on by the ministerial members of

the Annual Conference upon recommendation by the Board of Ordained Ministry. In every instance, with the exception of withdrawal to another denomination, the individual's membership moves from the Annual Conference to a local United Methodist church.

See also *administrative location of ordained ministers; location of clergy, honorable; church trials and trial procedures;* and *withdrawal of membership, ministerial.*

termination of local church membership (lay).

The removal of a lay person's membership in the local church. Membership in a local United Methodist church may be terminated by death, transfer to another United Methodist church, transfer to a church of another denomination, withdrawal of membership, expulsion as the consequence of a trial, or removal by action of the Charge Conference. It is the responsibility of the pastor of each local church or the membership secretary or both to maintain an accurate record of all terminations of membership.

See also *withdrawal of membership, ministerial; transfer, local church membership (lay); trials and trial procedures;* and *removal by Charge Conference action.*

testify, testimony.

The act of giving an account of or witnessing to one's faith in a public setting such as a prayer meeting, a study group, or a worship service. Testimony is used to refer to the content of what is said or written by the person testifying.

theological schools.

See *schools of theology.*

Theological Task, Our.

A brief essay printed in *The Book of Discipline* immediately preceding the Doctrinal Standards and General Rules. The current statement was adopted by the General Conference in 1988. "Our Theological Task" includes informative sections on the doctrinal heritage and affirmations of the Christian church and on the distinctive United Methodist heritage, including the Wesleyan emphases. "Our Theological Task" also contains an important section on United Methodist doctrinal history, including the doctrinal standards and traditions of American Methodism, the Evangelical United Brethren Church, and The United Methodist Church.

tithe. The setting aside of one-tenth of one's income for God as is specifically noted in the Bible. Tithing has been the traditional minimum standard of giving for Christians. The United Methodist Church has taken the official position that tithing is the standard for United Methodists, and the practice of tithing is to be actively encouraged in every local church.

title to church property.

See *trust clause in deeds*.

transept. The portions of the sanctuary that comprise the arms or the horizontal cross bar of the cross in those church buildings constructed in the shape of a cross.

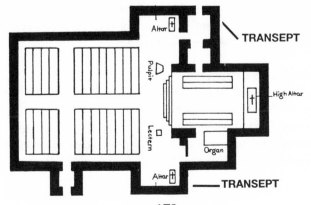

transfer, Annual Conference membership (ministerial).

The movement of the membership of ordained ministers from one Annual Conference to another. Although an ordained United Methodist minister is authorized to perform ministerial duties anywhere in the denomination, he or she is a member of only one Annual Conference. A minister may transfer from one Annual Conference to another with the approval of both of the bishops involved. Whenever possible, consultation with the chairperson or the executive committee of the Board of Ordained Ministry of the receiving Annual Conference should be held prior to the transfer.

transfer, local church membership (lay).

The movement of the membership of a lay person from one local church to another. A lay person may transfer his or her membership either to another United Methodist local church or to a local church of another denomination. The lay member does this by formally requesting that the pastor of the church to which he or she is transferring ask for the proper letter or certificate of transfer from the former church. When the letter or certificate of transfer is sent, the lay person ceases to be a member of the former local church.

trials and trial procedures.

See *church trials and trial procedures.*

trust clause in deeds.

The clause that must be included in the deeds of all United Methodist properties. All properties held by the General, Jurisdictional, Annual, and District Conferences or by a local church or by any agency or institution of the denomination are to be held in trust for the denomination.

The titles are not held by "The United Methodist Church" since it is a connectional structure and not a legal entity in and of itself. The titles to the properties are held by boards of trustees established for the purpose of holding and administering property. In the case of local churches, the deeds to all local churches, parsonages, and other properties must include a trust clause. This clause indicates that the property is to be maintained for the benefit of the local church as this ultimately relates to the ministry and work of the Annual Conference. When a local congregation disbands and services are discontinued, the property becomes the responsibility of the Annual Conference Board of Trustees. The property can be sold only after it is declared abandoned by a vote of the Annual Conference.

See also *abandon, local church.*

Trustees, Annual Conference Board of. The group of persons responsible for receiving, collecting, and holding in trust gifts and bequests given to the Annual Conference and for administering properties for which it has direct responsibility. The Annual Conference Board of Trustees consists of twelve persons elected by the Annual Conference. The Board of Trustees is to be incorporated.

Trustees, local church Board of. The group charged with the responsibility for the supervision and care of all property and equipment owned by the local church. The Board is to plan and set policies for the maintenance and use of the property and equipment, and receives and administers all bequests to the local church. The Board of Trustees consists of three to nine persons and at its discretion may be incorporated.

twelve-year rule. The regulation approved by the 1988 General Conference that no elected general program staff person can hold the same position for more than twelve years. Years of service prior to January 1, 1989, are not counted. In the general program agencies, the elected staff includes all persons with the rank or title of general secretary, deputy general secretary, associate general secretary, and assistant general secretary.

United Brethren in Christ.
See *Church of the United Brethren in Christ, The.*

United Methodist as trademark, use of.
The United States government regulation allowing The United Methodist Church to limit to official organizations the use of the words *Methodist* and *United Methodist*. As a result, these words are not to be used as a trade name or trademark or as a part of the name of any business or organization except for those specifically created for the administration of work undertaken by The United Methodist Church.

In addition, the "Cross and Flame" symbol of The United Methodist Church is a copyrighted, protected symbol. The specific shape and relative dimensions of the design of the symbol are clearly specified. It may not be used by any entity other than official United Methodist organizations without express written approval. United Methodist Communications is the agency responsible for supervising the use of this official insigne of The United Methodist Church.

United Methodist Church, The. This denomination was formed in 1968 by the union of The Evangelical United Brethren Church and The Methodist Church. It serves members in more than seventy Annual Conferences in five Jurisdictional Conferences in the United States and nearly forty Annual and Provisional Annual Conferences in seven Central Conferences in Africa, Europe, and the Philippines.

United Methodist Communications. The name used for the communication and public relations purposes of the General Commission on Communication. United Methodist Communications, established by the General Conference, provides leadership for The United Methodist Church in the fields of communication, public relations, and promotion of the funds and program of the denomination. It is the official news gathering and distribution agency of the denomination, and as such produces broadcast television, cable, and videotape programs and provides resources and services to local churches and Annual Conferences in the field of communications. It promotes the general funds and programs through *The Interpreter* and other means. Its offices are in Nashville, Tennessee.

The Book of Discipline also provides that there shall be a Committee on Communication in each Annual Conference to address these same purposes and issues.

United Methodist Men. The official organization for men in The United Methodist Church at the local church, Annual Conference, and denominational levels. Among the purposes for United Methodist Men are: (1) to involve men in a growing relationship to Jesus Christ and his church; (2) to provide resources and support for programs of evangelism focused on the needs of men; (3) to provide resources and programs in the area of stewardship; (4) to provide models and support for Annual Conference and local church United Methodist Men organizations. At the denominational level, United Methodist Men is a division of the General Board of Discipleship with offices in Nashville, Tennessee.

United Methodist Publishing House, The.
The name for the continuing work carried out and directed by the General Board of Publication. This agency, established by the General Conference, has the responsibility for and the supervision of the publishing interests of The United Methodist Church. The United Methodist Publishing House publishes and distributes all the official publications, records, and forms of the denomination, publishes books through Abingdon Press, and operates the Cokesbury retail stores and mail order service. It is also involved with the editorial development of church school materials, and it publishes and distributes church school materials and resources throughout the denomination. The offices of The United Methodist Publishing House are in Nashville, Tennessee.

United Methodist Reporter. A weekly newspaper widely circulated throughout the denomination. The newspaper focuses primarily on news and information items related to the various conferences and organizations of The United Methodist Church. It also provides news of other religious bodies and happenings. *The United Methodist Reporter* is circulated in a number of Annual Conference and local church editions. In these special editions, an Annual Conference or a local church may contract to have a page devoted to its news. *The United Methodist Reporter* is owned and published by the Texas Methodist Foundation. Its offices are in Dallas, Texas.

United Methodist Student Day. One of the special Sundays authorized by the General Conference to be observed with an offering on the Sunday after Thanksgiving. The purpose of United Methodist Student Day is to call upon the denomination to support United Methodist students as they prepare for life by adding knowledge to their faith. The funds received from the offering go into the United Methodist Student Loan Fund to underwrite scholarships for United Methodist students. The Fund is administered by the General Board of Higher Education and Ministry.

United Methodist Student Loan Fund. The fund established to assist United Methodist students to pay for undergraduate and graduate education. The loan fund is available upon application to qualified United Methodists. Upon repayment the funds are made available to other students. New monies come into the United Methodist Student Loan Fund through the offering taken in relation to the observance of United Methodist Student Day.

United Methodist Women. The official organization for women in The United Methodist Church at the local church, Annual Conference, and denominational levels. Among the purposes of United Methodist Women are the following: (1) to provide resources and opportunities for women that enrich their spiritual life and increase their knowledge of the needs of the world, (2) to enlist women in activities that have moral and religious significance for the public welfare and that contribute to the establishment of a just global society, (3) to secure funds for the support of the program of the church, with special concern for the needs and responsibilities of women, and (4) to project plans specifically directed toward leadership development of women. United Methodist Women is related to the Women's Division of the General Board of Global Ministries with offices in New York, New York.

United Methodist Youth. The programs and ministries for youth (generally persons in the seventh through the twelfth grades, of about twelve to eighteen years of age). The organization designed specifically for youth in the local church is known as the United Methodist Youth Fellowship.

United Methodist Youth Fellowship.
See *United Methodist Youth.*

University Senate. The professional educational advisory agency for The United Methodist Church and all educational institutions related to it. The University Senate represents those interests held in common by The United Methodist Church and its affiliated schools, colleges, universities, and graduate schools of theology. Among other tasks, the University Senate provides an effective review process for the educational institutions qualifying for affiliation with the denomination and for denominational support. The University Senate has twenty-five members elected by the General Conference and is related to the General Board of Higher Education and Ministry.

Upper Room, The. The daily devotional guide published for more than fifty years by the Upper Room division of the General Board of Discipleship. In addition to its wide distribution throughout the United States, *The Upper Room* is circulated to persons throughout the world in many language editions.

versicle. A short verse or sentence said or sung by a minister or worship leader and immediately followed with a response by the congregation. Versicles are also used by a choir and a congregation, two halves of a choir, or by a minister and a choir.

vesper service. A late afternoon or early evening service of worship.

vestments. Items of clothing such as robes, gowns, or other special garments and stoles worn by ministers and lay persons while conducting worship services.

vigil. A service or period of prayers and devotions usually held on the night before or in the early morning of important religious days or festivals. On occasion, special vigils are organized around a specific concern or issue in a local church. The word *vigil* comes from the Latin *vigilia,* meaning to watch.

vows, membership.
See *membership vows.*

W

wafer. The thin, circular disk of unleavened bread used in the Sacrament of the Lord's Supper. In some local United Methodist churches the wafer is used in place of ordinary bread for the sacrament.

See also *bread*.

Walk to Emmaus. A program of the Upper Room division of the General Board of Discipleship which calls forth and renews Christian discipleship. The Walk to Emmaus is a three-day experience, a highly structured weekend, which takes a New Testament look at Christianity as a life-style. The program is designed to strengthen and renew the faith of Christian people, and through them their families, congregations, and the world.

Watch Night Service.
See *Covenant Service, Wesley's*.

wedding ring. The ring or band given by the groom to the bride in the Service of Christian Marriage as a symbol of the wedding vows taken. In recent years it has become quite common for the bride also to give a ring to the groom. In the Service of Christian Marriage, the minister offers a prayer to bless the giving of the ring or rings.

Wesley, Charles. The younger brother of John Wesley and a formative leader in the Methodist movement. Charles Wesley (1707–1788) attended Christ College, Oxford, England, and was a founding member of the Holy Club. He was a missionary to Georgia, was deeply affected by the Moravian beliefs, and had a transforming religious experience in 1738, just a few days before his brother John. He was active through the remainder of his life in preaching and overseeing the growing Methodist work in England. His great contribution to the Wesleyan movement and to the entire Christian church was his hymns. He was a prolific writer of hymn poems and embodied much of the theology of Methodism in these poems.

Wesley, John. The founder of the Methodist movement. John Wesley (1703–1791) was born at Epworth, England, the son of a Church of England clergyman. He was graduated from Christ College, Oxford, England. For a brief period he was a missionary to Georgia. In 1738 he had an intense religious experience at a meeting on Aldersgate Street, London. Following this he began to preach throughout the country. He was a prolific preacher and writer, and his writings provided a core of standard doctrine and interpretation to guide the new Methodist movement. In 1784, he sent instructions to America for the formation of a separate Methodist church for the United States.

Wesleyan. The term that applies to those things related to John Wesley and the movement he began.

The word *Wesleyan* is in many ways synonymous with the word *Methodist*.

Wesley Quadrilateral, the. The phrase which has relatively recently come into use to describe the principal factors that John Wesley believed illuminate the core of the Christian faith for the believer. Wesley did not formulate the succinct statement now commonly referred to as the Wesley Quadrilateral. Building on the Anglican theological tradition, Wesley added a fourth emphasis, experience. The resulting four components or "sides" of the quadrilateral are (1) Scripture, (2) tradition, (3) reason, and (4) experience. For United Methodists, Scripture is considered the primary source and standard for Christian doctrine. Tradition is the

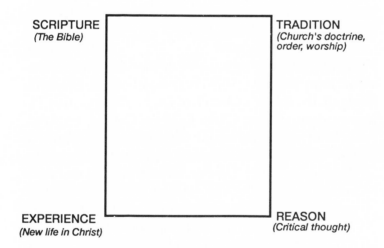

SCRIPTURE
(The Bible)

TRADITION
(Church's doctrine, order, worship)

EXPERIENCE
(New life in Christ)

REASON
(Critical thought)

WESLEY QUADRILATERAL

experience and the witness of the development and growth of the faith through the past centuries and in many nations and cultures. Experience is the individual's understanding and appropriating of the faith in the light of his or her own life. Through reason the individual Christian brings to bear on the Christian faith discerning and cogent thought. These four elements taken together bring the individual Christian to a mature and fulfilling understanding of the Christian faith and the required response of worship and service.

wine. The traditional term used by most Christian churches for the element used in the Sacrament of the Lord's Supper. The wine in the sacrament symbolizes the blood of Christ, which was shed for the redemption of all persons. Many denominations use the fermented juice of the grape or what is commonly referred to as wine. The United Methodist ritual for the Sacrament of the Lord's Supper refers to the communion elements as the bread and the wine. It has been the longstanding practice of United Methodism, however, to use only the unfermented juice of the grape.

withdrawal of membership, ministerial. The action on the part of the ministerial member of an Annual Conference to leave the membership. A minister may withdraw in order to join another denomination. In this instance, the minister surrenders his or her ministerial credentials to the Annual Conference. If the minister so desires, the credentials may be endorsed indicating that the minister honorably withdrew.

When a minister has been accused of an offense under the trial procedures of the denomination, under certain provisions the minister may elect and may be allowed to withdraw from the ministerial membership of the Conference. When this occurs the ministerial member surrenders his or her credentials to the Annual Conference.

Word and Table, Service of. The name approved and now used in *The United Methodist Hymnal* (1989) for the ritual that has traditionally been called the Sacrament of the Lord's Supper.

See also *Lord's Supper, Sacrament of the.*

words of assurance. The words spoken by the minister or other leader in a service of worship following a period of prayer and confession. Often they are taken from a passage of Scripture. The words of assurance are often a declaration of pardon and a statement of God's sustaining grace and love.

Words of Institution. The historical and traditional words that are a part of the ritual for the Sacrament of the Lord's Supper (now called Service of Word and Table). The Words of Institution are those which repeat the account and words of Jesus in the breaking of the bread and the sharing of the cup. These words are a part of what has traditionally been called the Prayer of Consecration. In the Services of Word and Table, as printed in *The United Methodist Hymnal* (1989), these Words of Institution are now a part of a section of the ritual entitled "The Great Thanksgiving," which must be said by an ordained minister.

work areas, local church. The organizations in the local church that provide for one or more persons to lead in ten significant subject areas. The Charge Conference is to elect a chairperson for each of these ten work areas annually. Larger congregations may have sizable work area committees, but small membership churches may have only a chairperson for each work area. The work areas report to the local church Council on Ministries or the Administrative Council. The ten local church work areas are Christian unity and interreligious concerns, church and society, education, evangelism, higher education and campus ministry, missions, religion and race, status and role of women, stewardship, and worship.

World Communion Sunday. One of the special Sundays authorized by the General Conference to be observed with the taking of an offering throughout the denomination. World Communion Sunday is observed on the first Sunday in October. The observance focuses the attention of United Methodists on the universal and inclusive nature of the church. One half of the proceeds from the offering is for Crusade Scholarships administered by the General Board of Global Ministries. The remaining one half is to be used for the Ethnic Scholarship Program and the Ethnic In-Service Training Program, which are administered by the General Board of Higher Education and Ministry.

World Council of Churches. A worldwide association of Christian churches. The United Methodist Church is a member. Its predecessor bodies, The Evangelical United Brethren Church and The Methodist Church, were charter members. United Methodists serve as members of the governing board and various units and committees of the World Council of Churches. Through the Interdenominational Cooperation Fund, The United Methodist Church contributes to the support of the World Council of Churches, whose headquarters are located in Geneva, Switzerland.

World Methodist Council. An organization comprising churches throughout the world that share a Wesleyan or Methodist heritage. The Evangelical United Brethren Church and The Methodist Church were charter members of the World Methodist Council. The United Methodist Church is a member. The United Methodist membership on the governing body of the Council is nominated by the Council of Bishops. United Methodist financial support for the World Methodist Council is provided through the Interdenominational Cooperation Fund. Its headquarters are located in Lake Junaluska, North Carolina.

World Service Fund. The basic general benevolence fund of The United Methodist Church. This fund is used to underwrite a large portion of the budgets and work of the general program agencies. The World Service Fund is deemed the first benevolent responsibility of the local United Methodist churches. The General Conference approves the amount to be raised each year for the World Service Fund. Each Annual Conference receives from the General Conference an apportionment of the amount for which it is responsible. By formula, each Annual Conference then determines the amount to be requested of each local church.

worship, local church work area on. The work area designed to assist the local church to become increasingly aware of the meaning, purpose, and practice of worship. The local church work area on worship is to work with the pastor, the music staff, and others to plan and care for the worship, music, furnishings, and other needs in order to facilitate the worship of the congregation.

195

Worship, The Book of. Contains resources to assist United Methodist ministers and other worship leaders in directing and facilitating the worship experiences in the local churches. *The Book of Worship* contains the orders of service and text for the official rituals and offices of The United Methodist Church. It also includes an anthology of Scripture readings, prayers, and other liturgical material, arranged according to the Christian year, to assist in the design of worship services. It includes a section consisting of the psalter and other acts of praise.

year, church. The official program and fiscal period used in The United Methodist Church for planning and administration. The General Conference has established the calendar year (January 1 through December 31) as the church year. The term of office for the officers in a local church is also the calendar year. The Christian calendar is followed for the observances of important Christian events and worship emphases.

See also *calendar, Christian.*

young adults. Those persons who are out of high school and nineteen through thirty years of age. This definition of young adults is used in The United Methodist Church as the basis for program development and implementation and for meeting the requirements for determining representatives to various organizations.

youth. Those persons from approximately twelve through eighteen years of age. This definition of youth is used in The United Methodist Church as the basis for program development and implementation and for meeting the representational requirements.

Youth Council, local church. Relates to all of
the local church's ministry with youth. The Youth
Council is to plan for and implement the programs with
and for youth. The Council is to keep the Council on
Ministries or the Administrative Council informed of
the needs for and the implementation of the programs
for youth. The membership of the Youth Council consists of the representatives from each local church work
area, adult leaders and counselors with youth, representative parents, and those related to youth programs.
In addition, the Youth Council is to have one youth
member for each adult member of the Council.

Youth Ministry, Annual Conference
Council on. The Annual Conference organization
whose purpose is to strengthen the youth ministry in
the local churches and districts. No more than one-third
of the membership of the Council on Youth Ministry
may be adults. This Council administers the Annual
Conference portion of the Youth Service Fund.

Youth Service Fund. The fund established to
serve as a means of stewardship education and support
of missions by youth within The United Methodist
Church. The youth in the local United Methodist
churches contribute to the Youth Service Fund. Of the
amount given, 70 percent is retained within the Annual
Conference to be administered by the Council on Youth
Ministry for projects it approves. The remaining 30 percent is forwarded to the National Youth Ministry Organization (NYMO) for the support of its program.

ACRONYMS AND ABBREVIATIONS IN USE IN THE UNITED METHODIST CHURCH

A

ABS	American Bible Society
AC	Annual Conference
ACBCS	Annual Conference Board of Church and Society
ACBGM	Annual Conference Board of Global Ministries
ACBOD	Annual Conference Board of Discipleship
ACBHECM	Annual Conference Board of Higher Education and Campus Ministry
ACBOP	Annual Conference Board of Pensions
ACCAH	Annual Conference Commission on Archives and History
ACCFA	Annual Conference Council on Finance and Administration
ACCOCUIC	Annual Conference Commission on Christian Unity and Interreligious Concerns
ACCOM	Annual Conference Council on Ministries

ACCORR	Annual Conference Commission on Religion and Race
ACCSRW	Annual Conference Commission on the Status and Role of Women
ACLL	Annual Conference Lay Leader
AGS	Associate General Secretary or Assistant General Secretary (of a general agency)
AM or A	Associate Member (Ministerial) in an Annual Conference
AME	The African Methodist Episcopal Church
AMEZ	The African Methodist Episcopal Church, Zion

B

BCS	Board of Church and Society
BDM	Board of Diaconal Ministry (Annual Conference)
BGM	Board of Global Ministries
BHEM	Board of Higher Education and Ministry
BMCR	Black Methodists for Church Renewal
BOD	Board of Discipleship
BOM	Board of Ordained Ministry (Annual Conference)

C

CAH	Commission on Archives and History
CC	Central Conference; Charge Conference or Church Conference
CCCA	Commission on Central Conference Affairs

CEF	Christian Educators Fellowship
CES	Commission on Equitable Salaries (Annual Conference)
CME	The Christian Methodist Episcopal Church
COB	Council of Bishops
COCU	The Consultation on Church Union
COCUIC	Commission on Church Union and Interreligious Concerns
COM	Council on Ministries
CORR	Commission on Religion and Race
CRC	Curriculum Resources Committee
CSP	Church School Publications
CSRW or COSROW	Commission on the Status and Role of Women
CYM	Council on Youth Ministries

D

DACCOM or DCOM	Director of the Annual Conference Council on Ministries
DC	District Conference
DCA	*Daily Christian Advocate*
DCOM	District Council on Ministries
DLL	District Lay Leader
DM	Diaconal Minister
DS	District Superintendent

E

E	Elder or Full Member (Ministerial) of Annual Conference

EA	The Evangelical Association
EC	The Evangelical Church
ELC	Ethnic Local Church
EUB	The Evangelical United Brethren Church

F

FM or F	Full Member (Ministerial) of Annual Conference

G

GAF	General Administration Fund
GBCS	General Board of Church and Society
GBGM	General Board of Global Ministries
GBHEM	General Board of Higher Education and Ministry
GBOD	General Board of Discipleship
GBPB	General Board of Publication
GBPN	General Board of Pensions
GC	General Conference (rarely used)
GCAH	General Commission on Archives and History
GCFA	General Council on Finance and Administration
GCOC	General Commission on Communication
GCOCUIC	General Commission on Church Union and Interreligious Concerns
GCOM	General Council on Ministries
GCORR	General Commission on Religion and Race

GCSRW	General Commission on the Status and Role of Women
GS	General Secretary (of a general agency)

H

I

ICE	Interjurisdictional Committee on the Episcopacy
ICF	Interdenominational Cooperation Fund

J

JAC	Jurisdictional Administrative Council
JC	Jurisdictional Conference
JCAH	Jurisdictional Commission on Archives and History
JCCOM	Jurisdictional Conference Council on Ministries
JCE	Jurisdictional Committee on the Episcopacy
JCUMM	Jurisdictional Committee on United Methodist Men
JUMW	Jurisdictional United Methodist Women
JYMO	Jurisdictional Youth Ministry Organization

K

L

LCCOM	Local Church Council on Ministries
LL	Lay Leader
LP	Local Pastor

M

MARCHA	Metodistas Asociados Representado la Causa de los Hispano Americanos (Methodists Associated Representing the Cause of Hispanic Americans)
MC	The Methodist Church
MEC	The Methodist Episcopal Church
MECS	The Methodist Episcopal Church, South
MEF	Ministerial Education Fund
MFSA	Methodist Federation for Social Action
MP	The Methodist Protestant Church

N

NAACLL	National Association of Annual Conference Lay Leaders
NACCD	National Association of Conference Council Directors
NAIC	Native American International Caucus
NCCC	National Council of the Churches of Christ in the U.S.A.
NCJ	North Central Jurisdiction
NEJ	Northeastern Jurisdiction
NFAAUM	National Fellowship of Asian American United Methodists
NYMO	National Youth Ministry Organization

O

OM	Ordained Minister

P

PM	Probationary Member (ministerial) of an Annual Conference
PPR	Pastor-Parish Relations Committee (local church)

Q

QR	*Quarterly Review* (a magazine)

R

RT or R	Retired Member (ministerial) of an Annual Conference

S

SCJ	South Central Jurisdiction
SEJ	Southeastern Jurisdiction

T

U

UB	The Church of the United Brethren in Christ
UMATS	United Methodist Association of Theological Schools
UMC	The United Methodist Church
UMCom	United Methodist Communications
UMCOR	United Methodist Committee on Relief
UMM	United Methodist Men
UMNYMO	United Methodist National Youth Ministry Organization

UMPH	The United Methodist Publishing House
UMW	United Methodist Women

V

W

WCC	World Council of Churches
WJ	Western Jurisdiction
WMC	World Methodist Council
WSCB	World Service and Conference Benevolences
WSF	World Service Fund

X

Y

YSF	Youth Service Fund

Z

REFERENCE MATERIALS FOR ADDITIONAL READING

The Book of Discipline of The United Methodist Church. (Nashville: The United Methodist Publishing House, 1988).

The Book of Resolutions of The United Methodist Church (Nashville: The United Methodist Publishing House, 1988).

The Encyclopedia of World Methodism, vols. 1 and 2, Nolan B. Harmon, general ed. (Nashville: The United Methodist Publishing House, 1974).

Faith and Form: A Unity of Theology and Polity in the United Methodist Tradition, Robert L. Wilson and Steve Harper (Grand Rapids, Mich.: Zondervan, 1988).

Handbook of the Christian Year, Hoyt L. Hickman, Don E. Saliers, Laurence Hull Stookey, and James F. White (Nashville: Abingdon Press, 1986).

The Hymns of The United Methodist Hymnal (Introduction to the Hymns, Canticles, and Acts of Worship), Diana Sanchez, vol. ed. (Nashville: Abingdon Press, 1989).

The Organization of The United Methodist Church (1989 ed.), Jack M. Tuell (Nashville: Abingdon Press, 1989).

The Story of American Methodism, Frederick A. Norwood (Nashville/New York: Abingdon Press, 1974).

Understanding The United Methodist Church (rev. ed.), Nolan B. Harmon (Nashville: Abingdon, 1977).

Wesleyan Theology, A Sourcebook, Thomas A. Langford (Durham, N.C.: Labyrinth Press, 1984).

The Worship Resources of The United Methodist Hymnal (Introduction to the General Services, Psalter, and Other Acts of Worship), Hoyt L. Hickman, vol. ed. (Nashville: Abingdon Press, 1989).